Apress Pocket Guides

Apress Pocket Guides present concise summaries of cutting-edge developments and working practices throughout the tech industry. Shorter in length, books in this series aims to deliver quick-to-read guides that are easy to absorb, perfect for the time-poor professional.

This series covers the full spectrum of topics relevant to the modern industry, from security, AI, machine learning, cloud computing, web development, product design, to programming techniques and business topics too.

Typical topics might include:

- A concise guide to a particular topic, method, function or framework

- Professional best practices and industry trends

- A snapshot of a hot or emerging topic

- Industry case studies

- Concise presentations of core concepts suited for students and those interested in entering the tech industry

- Short reference guides outlining 'need-to-know' concepts and practices.

More information about this series at `https://link.springer.com/bookseries/17385`.

IAM and PAM Cybersecurity

Securing Identities and
Access Management
in the Digitalization Era

Massimo Nardone

Apress®

IAM and PAM Cybersecurity: Securing Identities and Access Management in the Digitalization Era

Massimo Nardone
Helsinki, Finland

ISBN-13 (pbk): 979-8-8688-2018-2 ISBN-13 (electronic): 979-8-8688-2019-9
https://doi.org/10.1007/979-8-8688-2019-9

Copyright © 2025 by Massimo Nardone

This work is subject to copyright. All rights are reserved by the Publisher, whether the whole or part of the material is concerned, specifically the rights of translation, reprinting, reuse of illustrations, recitation, broadcasting, reproduction on microfilms or in any other physical way, and transmission or information storage and retrieval, electronic adaptation, computer software, or by similar or dissimilar methodology now known or hereafter developed.

Trademarked names, logos, and images may appear in this book. Rather than use a trademark symbol with every occurrence of a trademarked name, logo, or image we use the names, logos, and images only in an editorial fashion and to the benefit of the trademark owner, with no intention of infringement of the trademark.

The use in this publication of trade names, trademarks, service marks, and similar terms, even if they are not identified as such, is not to be taken as an expression of opinion as to whether or not they are subject to proprietary rights.

While the advice and information in this book are believed to be true and accurate at the date of publication, neither the authors nor the editors nor the publisher can accept any legal responsibility for any errors or omissions that may be made. The publisher makes no warranty, express or implied, with respect to the material contained herein.

    Managing Director, Apress Media LLC: Welmoed Spahr
    Acquisitions Editor: Susan McDermott
    Development Editor: Laura Berendson
    Project Manager: Jessica Vakili

Distributed to the book trade worldwide by Springer Science+Business Media New York, 1 New York Plaza, New York, NY 10004. Phone 1-800-SPRINGER, fax (201) 348-4505, e-mail orders-ny@springer-sbm.com, or visit www.springeronline.com. Apress Media, LLC is a Delaware LLC and the sole member (owner) is Springer Science + Business Media Finance Inc (SSBM Finance Inc). SSBM Finance Inc is a **Delaware** corporation.

For information on translations, please e-mail booktranslations@springernature.com; for reprint, paperback, or audio rights, please e-mail bookpermissions@springernature.com.

Apress titles may be purchased in bulk for academic, corporate, or promotional use. eBook versions and licenses are also available for most titles. For more information, reference our Print and eBook Bulk Sales web page at http://www.apress.com/bulk-sales.

Any source code or other supplementary material referenced by the author in this book is available to readers on the Github repository: https://github.com/Apress/IAM-and-PAM-Cybersecurity. For more detailed information, please visit https://www.apress.com/gp/services/source-code.

If disposing of this product, please recycle the paper

Table of Contents

About the Author ix

Chapter 1: IAM, Securing Identities in the Digitalization Era 1
    The Importance of Securing Identities in the Digitalization Era 2
    What Is Identity Access Management (IAM)? 5
    Why Considering IAM Is Crucial? 7
    What Are the IAM Key Components? 10
    What the Key Security IAM Features Are? 13
    Which Are the Best Practices for IAM Implementation? 19
    Introduction of IAM in Cloud Platforms 23
    Advanced Insights into Key IAM Features: Industry Applications and Future Trends 28
    Future Trends in IAM 30
    Summary 32

Chapter 2: PAM, Protecting Privileged Accounts and Access Management 33
    The Evolution of Access Management 34
    Trends Shaping Access Management Today 36
    What Is the Critical Role of Access Management in Cybersecurity? 38
    Challenges Specific to Cybersecurity 39
    Emerging Technologies Enhancing Cybersecurity in Access Management 40
    Best Practices for Cybersecurity-Focused Access Management 41

TABLE OF CONTENTS

The Future of Access Management in Cybersecurity 41

User Accounts and Privileged Accounts: Key Pillars of Cybersecurity Management 43

User Accounts Introduction 44

Privileged Accounts Introduction 44

Understanding User Accounts and Privileged Accounts in Cybersecurity 49

Privileged Accounts: Gatekeepers of Critical Resources 50

Why Are Privileged Accounts Critical? 50

The Importance of Zero Trust in Privileged Account Security 51

What Is Zero Trust? 52

The Five Core Principles of Zero Trust 53

What the Most Common Key Zero Trust Strategies Are? 55

How Zero Trust Works? 57

What Is Privileged Access Management (PAM)? 58

Privileged Accounts vs. Privileged Access 59

Traditional PAM: Core Functions and Tools 60

Key Functional Categories in PAM 60

Privileged Credential Management 62

Why PAM Is Important? 62

PAM vs. PIM 63

PAM vs. IAM 63

PAM and the Principle of Least Privilege 64

Challenges with Traditional PAM in the Cloud 64

Key Differences Between IT and OT Privileged Access Management (PAM) 65

Most Common PAM Vendors for IT Environments 69

Most Common PAM Vendors for OT Environments 70

Summary 72

TABLE OF CONTENTS

Chapter 3: IAM and PAM Risks, Impacts, and Challenges 75

Risks, Impacts, and Operational Challenges Associated with IAM and
PAM in Modern Cybersecurity 81

What Are the Most Common IAM and PAM Cybersecurity Impacts? 83

What Was the NotPetya Malware Attack? 90

What Are the Most Common IAM and PAM Challenges? 91

Examples of Cybersecurity Attacks Involving IAM and PAM Systems 94

Introducing MITRE Att&ck 95

Main MITRE ATT&CK Matrices 96

Example 1: The Capital One Data Breach (2019) 100

Example 2: Hypothetical Cyberattack Scenario in a Manufacturing Plant 102

Example 3: Manufacturing Industry Cyberattack Scenario: Breach via
Poor IAM & PAM Controls 105

The Future of Identity and Access Management (IAM) and Privileged
Access Management (PAM) 108

Summary 109

Chapter 4: IAM and PAM Tools, Standards and Frameworks 111

Introduction to IAM and PAM Tools 112

Introduction to IAM and PAM Tools Vendors 117

Introduction to IAM and PAM Frameworks 122

Pros and Cons of IAM and PAM Frameworks 125

Implementing IAM and PAM Standards 131

Summary 136

About the Author

Massimo Nardone has more than 30 years of experience in information and cybersecurity for IT/OT/IoT/IIoT, web/mobile development, cloud, and IT architecture. His true IT passions are security and Android. He holds an M.Sc. degree in computing science from the University of Salerno, Italy.

Throughout his working career, he has held various positions starting as Programming Developer, then Security Teacher, PCI QSA, Auditor, Assessor, Lead IT/OT/SCADA/Cloud Architect, CISO, BISO, Executive, Program Director, OT/IoT/IIoT Security Competence Leader, etc. In his last working engagement, he worked as a seasoned Cyber and Information Security Executive, CISO, and OT, IoT, and IIoT Security Competence Leader, helping many clients to develop and implement Cyber, Information, OT, and IoT Security activities.

He is currently working as Vice President of OT Security for SSH Communications Security.

He is a co-author of numerous Apress books, including *Spring Security 6 Recipes, Secure RESTful APIs, Cybersecurity Threats and Attacks in the Gaming Industry, Pro Spring Security, Beginning EJB in Java EE 8, Pro JPA 2 in Java EE 8*, and *Pro Android Games*, and has reviewed more than 100 titles.

CHAPTER 1

IAM, Securing Identities in the Digitalization Era

In today's digital world, organizations face an increasing number of cyber threats targeting user identities and access credentials.

Identity and Access Management (IAM) plays a crucial role in securing identities, managing user privileges, and enforcing security policies across enterprise environments. As cloud adoption, remote work, and IoT expand, IAM has become essential for ensuring zero-trust security, regulatory compliance, and operational efficiency.

We must understand well the main difference between IAM and Privileged Access Management (PAM), which is a specialized cybersecurity framework that focuses on securing, monitoring, and managing privileged accounts and access rights in an organization. Privileged accounts, such as administrators, root users, and service accounts, have elevated access to critical systems, making them prime targets for cyberattacks.

Both IAM (Identity and Access Management) and PAM (Privileged Access Management) are cybersecurity frameworks designed to control and protect user access to systems, applications, and data. They play a crucial role in IoT security, cloud security, and enterprise cybersecurity by preventing unauthorized access and mitigating insider threats.

CHAPTER 1   IAM, SECURING IDENTITIES IN THE DIGITALIZATION ERA

This pocket book is an introductory guide to IAM and PAM security, covering key topics like securing identities in the digitalization era, key elements of protecting privileged accounts and access management, the major IAM and PAM risks, impacts, and challenges, and finally the most commonly used IAM and PAM tools and frameworks.

The Importance of Securing Identities in the Digitalization Era

In today's digital age, the rapid transformation of how we live, work, and interact relies heavily on digital identities. As more services, transactions, and communications move online, securing these identities becomes critically important.

Digital identities are the digital footprints that authenticate and authorize users to access various platforms and data. If these identities are compromised, it can lead to severe consequences such as financial loss, data breaches, identity theft, and erosion of trust. Cybercriminals increasingly target digital identities because they serve as gateways to sensitive information and assets.

Furthermore, as organizations adopt technologies like cloud computing, IoT, and AI, the attack surface expands, making robust identity security essential for safeguarding privacy and maintaining regulatory compliance. Strong identity verification processes, multi-factor authentication, and continuous monitoring help prevent unauthorized access and ensure the integrity of digital interactions.

Securing digital identities is a foundational aspect of the digital era. It safeguards sensitive data, prevents financial and reputational damage, ensures regulatory compliance, and forms the backbone of trustworthy digital ecosystems. As the digital landscape continues to evolve, investing in robust identity security measures is vital for enabling safe, innovative, and resilient digital environments.

We must understand the following elements when dealing with why securing identities in the digitalization era:

- **Increasing Volume and Value of Data**

    Digital identities often include sensitive information such as personal details, financial data, health records, and proprietary business information. Cybercriminals recognize the high value of this data, and compromised identities can be exploited for fraudulent activities, identity theft, and financial crimes. Securing identities helps prevent unauthorized access and data breaches.

- **Expanding Threat Landscape**

    Gone are the days when threats were limited to simple malware or viruses. Today's cyber threats involve complex tactics like phishing, social engineering, account hijacking, and credential stuffing. These attacks specifically target weak or compromised digital identities, making robust identity security measures essential.

- **Critical for Trust and Credibility**

    Reliable digital identities foster trust among users, customers, and partners. For example, secure online banking relies on strong authentication methods to reassure users their assets are protected. Conversely, breaches can lead to loss of reputation, legal repercussions, and diminished consumer confidence.

- **Compliance with Regulations**

  Governments and regulatory bodies worldwide have implemented strict data protection laws such as GDPR, HIPAA, and CCPA. Organizations must implement effective identity security protocols to comply with these regulations, avoid hefty fines, and protect user privacy.

- **Enabling Secure Digital Transactions and Services**

  As automation, online shopping, remote work, and digital payments become the norm, secure identity verification ensures that only authorized individuals access sensitive services. Multi-factor authentication, biometric verification, and passwordless security solutions enhance security and reduce fraud.

- **Supporting Future Technologies**

  Emerging technologies like IoT, AI, and blockchain heavily depend on secure identities for seamless operation. For instance, IoT devices require trusted identities to communicate securely, and blockchain relies on verifiable digital identities to maintain transparency and trust.

Securing digital identities is not merely an operational necessity but a strategic imperative in the digitalization era. It underpins trust, safeguards assets, facilitates compliance, and enables innovation. Effective IAM and PAM are essential components in building resilient, secure, and trustworthy digital ecosystems.

Let's understand now better what is Identity Access Management (IAM).

What Is Identity Access Management (IAM)?

IAM stands for Identity and Access Management. It is a framework of policies, technologies, and processes used to securely manage digital identities and control access to resources within an organization. IAM ensures that the right individuals have appropriate access to technology resources, such as applications, data, and infrastructure, while preventing unauthorized access. Common components of IAM include user authentication, authorization, password management, and role-based access control.

IAM is fundamental for protecting organizational assets, maintaining regulatory compliance, ensuring operational efficiency, and delivering a good user experience.

IAM general elements are as follows:

User Management

- Establishing and configuring user roles within the organization

- Defining the specific permissions and access levels for each user or group within the system

- Applying the relevant roles for new employees upon joining the company

- Ensuring timely and appropriate role changes when employees transition to different positions or departments

- Deleting or modifying roles when an employee exits the company, ensuring no residual access remains

CHAPTER 1   IAM, SECURING IDENTITIES IN THE DIGITALIZATION ERA

Authentication

- Verifying the identity of users accessing the system
- Implementing Multi-factor authentication (MFA)
- Implementing biometric or token-based authentication
- Continuously updating authentication methods to combat evolving security threats and vulnerabilities

Authorization

- Governing the access privileges granted to the users
- Role-Based Access Control (RBAC) to assign specific permissions based on predefined roles
- Attribute-Based Access Control (ABAC) to adjust access based on contextual and environmental factors
- Strict business policies to ensure that only authorized individuals access critical assets under appropriate circumstances

Directory Services

- A centralized source for user information and configurations
- Single Sign-On (SSO) by storing user data required for seamless authentication across multiple platforms
- Interoperability with diverse identity systems to streamline user management and access control
- Housing all user-related data in a centralized and easily accessible location

IAM general elements are shown in Figure 1-1.

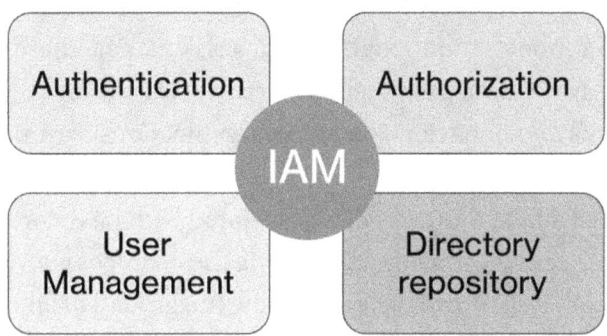

Figure 1-1. *IAM general elements*

Common IAM Technologies and Solutions include the following:

- **Identity providers (IdPs)** like Microsoft Azure AD, Okta, and Ping Identity.

- **Federated identity management** for single sign-on across multiple systems.

- **Privileged access management (PAM)** for controlling high-level accounts.

Why Considering IAM Is Crucial?

Considering Identity and Access Management (IAM) is crucial because it enhances security by ensuring that only authorized users have access to sensitive information, thus preventing unauthorized access and breaches. It helps organizations comply with regulatory and industry standards, such as GDPR and HIPAA, thereby reducing legal and financial risks. IAM also streamlines user management processes, increasing operational efficiency by reducing the time and effort needed to handle accounts and access rights.

Furthermore, IAM improves user experience through features like Single Sign-On (SSO), allowing users to log in once and access multiple systems, which boosts productivity. From a risk management perspective, IAM identifies and manages potential security risks by monitoring access patterns and behaviors, enabling organizations to mitigate risks proactively.

Additionally, IAM reduces costs associated with password resets and manual access provisioning by automating these processes, making it cost-effective. It is also scalable, supporting the growth of an organization by efficiently managing identities and access in large and complex environments. Finally, IAM ensures accountability by providing detailed logs and audit trails, making it possible to trace access and actions taken within systems. Implementing effective IAM practices is essential for protecting data, meeting compliance requirements, and facilitating smoother operations and user interactions.

To simply summarize, IAM is very important for the following reasons:

- **Security:** Reduces the risk of unauthorized access, data breaches, and insider threats.

- **Efficiency:** Automates user provisioning, de-provisioning, and access workflows.

- **Compliance:** Helps organizations adhere to standards such as GDPR, HIPAA, and others.

- **User Experience:** Simplifies login processes through SSO and MFA, improving productivity.

Let's elaborate the critical reasons to implement IAM.

1. **Enhances Security:**
    - Proper IAM measures prevent unauthorized access, reducing the risk of data breaches, insider threats, and cyberattacks.

CHAPTER 1   IAM, SECURING IDENTITIES IN THE DIGITALIZATION ERA

- It ensures that only verified and authorized users can access sensitive systems and data.

2. **Ensures Regulatory Compliance:**

    - Many industries are subject to regulations (like GDPR, HIPAA, and PCI DSS) that require strict access controls and audit trails.

    - IAM helps organizations meet these compliance standards by providing secure, auditable access management.

3. **Reduces Risk of Insider Threats:**

    - IAM controls who can access what, minimizing the chances of malicious or accidental data leaks and misuse.

    - Role-based and status-based access controls limit privileges to the minimum necessary.

4. **Streamlines User Management:**

    - Automated workflows for onboarding, offboarding, and updating user permissions save time and reduce errors.

    - Simplifies password resets, account provisioning, and deprovisioning processes.

5. **Improves User Experience:**

    - Single Sign-On (SSO) and Multi-Factor Authentication (MFA) make login processes more convenient and secure for users.

    - Reduces password fatigue and support requests related to login issues.

6. **Supports Digital Transformation:**
   - As organizations adopt cloud services, remote work, and mobile access, IAM provides a unified way to manage access across diverse environments.
   - Facilitates secure integration of new technologies and platforms.

7. **Prevents Data Loss and Downtime:**
   - Proper access controls can prevent accidental or malicious destruction or modification of data.
   - Ensures critical systems remain secure and operational with controlled access.

8. **Monitoring and Audit:**
   - Tracking password resets and modifications
   - Identifying and managing orphan accounts
   - Monitoring privileged account activities
   - Tracking the number and types of roles associated with each user or account
   - Detecting and addressing separation of duties (SoD) violations
   - Monitoring nonhuman identities (service accounts)

What Are the IAM Key Components?

Identity and Access Management (IAM) is a critical framework for managing digital identities and controlling access to resources within an organization. Its key components include identification, which involves assigning unique identifiers to users or systems. Authentication follows, ensuring that these identities are verified using methods like passwords or multi-factor authentication. Once authenticated, authorization determines what resources and actions the user or system can access or perform.

IAM also encompasses roles and policies, which define specific access levels and permissions for users and groups, facilitating efficient resource management. User management is an essential part of IAM, involving the creation, modification, and deletion of user accounts and profiles.

Another critical component is access control, which implements rules that restrict or permit access to resources. Audit and monitoring provide logging of access and usage activities, crucial for security and compliance purposes.

IAM manages the entire lifecycle of user identities, from creation to termination, ensuring that access is appropriately granted and revoked. It often includes federated identity management, enabling users to use a single set of credentials across multiple systems. Single Sign-On (SSO), a feature of IAM, enhances user experience by allowing access to multiple applications with one login. These components collectively enhance security, ensure compliance, and improve operational efficiency.

The Key Components of IAM are as follows:

- **Users**: Employees, Contractors, Customers, Partners.
- **Access Management**:
    - **Authentication:**
        - Verifying the identity of users trying to access systems.
        - Common methods include passwords, biometrics, multi-factor authentication (MFA), and single sign-on (SSO).

- **Authorization:**
  - Determining what resources a user can access and what actions they can perform.
  - Typically implemented through role-based access control (RBAC), attribute-based access control (ABAC), or policy-based access control.
- **SSO**
- **Access Governance:**
  - Ensuring compliance with policies and regulations.
  - Monitoring and auditing user activity to prevent misuse or data breaches.
- **Identity Management:**
  - Creation, maintenance, and deletion of user identities.
  - Managing user attributes such as roles, permissions, and profiles.
  - Ensuring that user identities are unique and verified.
  - Managing user accounts from onboarding to offboarding.
  - Automating permission adjustments as roles or statuses change.
  - Enforcing strong password policies.
  - Facilitating password resets and recovery processes.
- **Resources**: Applications, Platforms, Data resources, etc.

The IAM key components are shown in Figure 1-2.

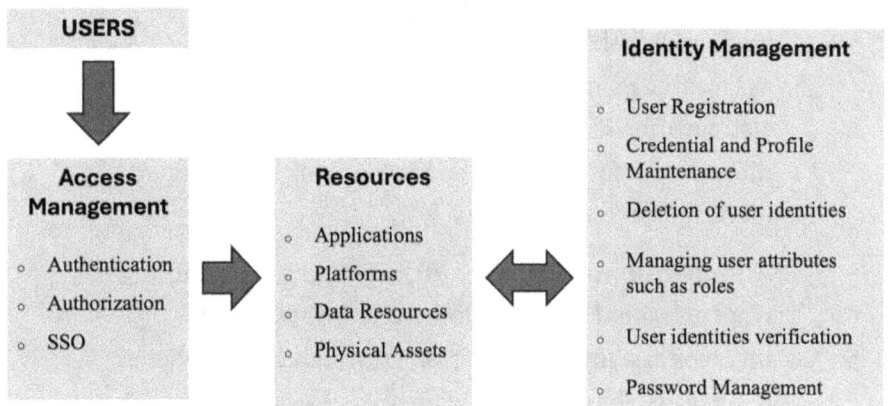

Figure 1-2. *IAM key components*

What the Key Security IAM Features Are?

In modern digital environments, safeguarding access to sensitive systems and data is paramount. Central to this effort are the core features of Identity and Access Management (IAM), which work collectively to verify user identities, control permissions, and enhance security while delivering seamless user experiences. Among these, Authentication and Authorization, Single Sign-On (SSO), and Multi-Factor Authentication (MFA) play crucial roles. Let's elaborate those.

- **Authentication:** It is the foundational process that establishes a user's identity. Traditionally, authentication relied heavily on straightforward methods such as usernames and passwords, but today's security landscape demands more robust mechanisms. Modern systems employ multi-factor authentication, biometrics (fingerprints, facial recognition), hardware tokens, smart cards, and digital certificates to verify identities.

The idea is to ensure that the user is genuinely who they claim to be, minimizing the risk of impersonation or credential theft. Advanced authentication protocols such as OAuth, OpenID Connect, and SAML facilitate secure, standardized exchanges of authentication data across different platforms and services, allowing for federated identity scenarios.

- **Authorization:** It follows authentication, determining what a verified user can do within the system. It involves assigning permissions through roles, policies, or attribute-based access control (ABAC). Role-Based Access Control (RBAC) is common, where permissions are grouped into roles (e.g., admin, user, guest), and users are assigned roles accordingly. Attribute-Based Access Control (ABAC) goes further by granting access based on attributes such as user department, location, or device type. Fine-grained authorization ensures that users only access data and perform actions aligned with their privileges, reducing the risk of data breaches and enforcing compliance.

- **Single Sign-On (SSO):** It is a transformative feature that enhances user productivity and reduces credential management burdens. With SSO, a user authenticates once using a centralized identity provider (IdP) and gains access to multiple connected applications and services without repeated logins. This not only simplifies the user experience but also reduces password fatigue, which is a common cause of weak password practices. SSO leverages standards like SAML, OAuth, and OpenID Connect for secure token exchanges. Implementing SSO requires careful configuration to ensure that token securely carries authentication assertions and that sessions are managed properly to prevent vulnerabilities such as session hijacking. An example of how SSO works is shown in Figure 1-3.

Figure 1-3. *IAM SSO flow*

Typical **IAM Single Sign-On (SSO)** applications are those that benefit from centralized authentication to improve security, user experience, and administrative efficiency. These applications span IT, business, and operational domains—especially in industries like manufacturing where users interact with a diverse set of systems.

Here's a categorized list:

Enterprise and Productivity Tools:

- Microsoft 365/Office 365
- Google Workspace
- Salesforce
- Slack, Microsoft Teams
- Zoom, WebEx

ERP, SCM, and Business Systems:

- SAP (S/4HANA, ECC)
- Oracle ERP Cloud
- Infor
- NetSuite
- Microsoft Dynamics 365

HR and Identity Systems:

- Workday
- SuccessFactors
- ADP
- BambooHR
- UKG (Ultimate Kronos Group)

IT Infrastructure and Developer Tools:

- AWS, Azure, Google Cloud Platform (GCP)
- GitHub, GitLab, Bitbucket
- Jenkins, Ansible, Terraform
- ServiceNow
- Jira, Confluence

Manufacturing and Industrial Systems:

- MES (Manufacturing Execution Systems) platforms
- SCADA/HMI dashboards (with modern identity support)
- IoT/IIoT platforms (e.g., PTC ThingWorx, Siemens MindSphere)

- PLM systems (e.g., Siemens Teamcenter, PTC Windchill)
- CAD/CAM software (e.g., AutoCAD, SolidWorks—cloud versions)

Security and Compliance Tools:

- SIEM systems (e.g., Splunk, IBM QRadar)
- Endpoint protection platforms (e.g., CrowdStrike, SentinelOne)
- DLP, CASB, and PAM solutions
- Compliance management tools (e.g., Vanta, LogicGate)

Customer-Facing or Partner Portals:

- Supplier portals
- B2B e-commerce platforms
- Customer support portals
- Extranets for partners/distributors
- **Multi-Factor Authentication (MFA):** It adds an essential layer of security by requiring users to verify their identity through two or more different factors. These factors typically fall into three categories: something you know (password, PIN), something you have (security token, mobile device), and something you are (biometric data). Combining multiple factors makes it significantly harder for attackers to gain unauthorized access, even if they compromise one factor. MFA solutions range from simple SMS codes to sophisticated biometric verification, and many organizations integrate MFA with adaptive

authentication. Adaptive MFA dynamically adjusts authentication requirements based on contextual risk factors, such as login location, device, or network conditions, thus balancing security with usability.

Here is a list of how IAM MFA generally works step by step:

1. **User Login Attempt**

   The user enters their **username and password** on an application or system login page.

2. **First Factor—Something You Know**

   The system verifies the **password** (knowledge-based factor).

3. **Triggering Second Factor**

   Once the password is verified, the IAM system prompts for a **second authentication method**.

4. **Second Factor—Something You Have/Are**

   The user must verify their identity using one of the following:

   - **Something you have**:
     - Mobile phone app (e.g., Microsoft Authenticator, Google Authenticator)
     - Hardware token (e.g., YubiKey)
     - SMS or email with a one-time passcode (OTP)
     - Push notification for approval
   - **Something you are**:
     - Biometric verification (fingerprint, facial recognition)

5. **Authentication Server Validation**

    The IAM system checks the second factor via its MFA service. If valid, the user is authenticated.

6. **Access Granted**

    Upon successful multi-factor verification, access is granted to the system or application.

Deploying these features as part of a comprehensive IAM strategy enables organizations to protect themselves against evolving cyber threats, comply with regulatory requirements, and provide users with a secure, seamless experience across all digital touchpoints. Achieving this integration requires careful planning, adherence to best practices, and continuous monitoring to adapt to new security challenges and technological advancements.

In essence, these features are interconnected and mutually reinforcing. Authentication and Authorization establish and enforce user identities and privileges. SSO delivers convenience without compromising security by centralizing authentication. MFA elevates security standards by providing multiple verification layers, drastically reducing the likelihood of successful breaches.

Which Are the Best Practices for IAM Implementation?

Implementing Identity and Access Management (IAM) effectively is essential for safeguarding an organization's digital assets, ensuring regulatory compliance, and enabling seamless user experiences. As modern IT environments grow increasingly complex—with hybrid infrastructures, cloud adoption, and remote work—robust IAM practices become more critical than ever. A well-structured IAM strategy helps ensure that only the right individuals have appropriate access to the right resources at the right time. This document outlines industry best practices for IAM implementation, providing a framework to strengthen security, streamline access control, and support organizational agility.

Let's have a look at the most important best practices for IAM Implementation.

Embrace a Zero Trust Approach to Security:

Implicit trust in applications and tools can jeopardize security. Adopting a zero-trust model ensures constant user verification before granting access to company resources.

- Implement Zero Trust principles: never trust, always verify; assume breach; and least-privileged access.

- Synergize IAM tools with Zero Trust architecture for rigorous user authentication, reducing risks of unauthorized access.

Identify and Safeguard High-Value Data:

Securing crucial data starts with limiting access. Recognize high-value assets, assess where they're stored, and apply access control policies to ensure data security.

- Identify sensitive data like trade secrets or personal information.

- Utilize Azure, GCP, and AWS IAM practices to safeguard cloud-stored data.

Enforce a Robust Password Policy:

Strong passwords and unique authentication are vital. Regularly review password strength and employ Multi-Factor Authentication (MFA) for added security layers.

- Ensure complex, unique passwords for each user.

- Implement enhanced password protocols.

Implement Multi-Factor Authentication (MFA):
Validating a user's identity is crucial. MFA tools provide multiple validation steps, ensuring authorized access.

- Utilize biometric, possession, and knowledge authentication methods.
- Enhance security with layered authentication.

Automate Workflows:
IAM tools facilitate automation for enhanced security, reducing manual errors, and aiding compliance needs.

- Automate tasks like account creation and access provisioning.
- Simplify compliance reporting through automated logs.

Embrace the Least Privilege Principle:
Limit access as much as possible without impeding workflows, employing role-based and attribute-based access controls.

- Define minimum privilege levels for each role.
- Regularly audit and reduce unnecessary permissions.

Implement Just-in-Time Access:
For temporarily elevated privileges, employ just-in-time access, ensuring granular and controlled access.

- Temporarily elevate permissions without compromising security.
- Ideal for external users requiring periodic access.

Utilize RBAC and ABAC Policies:
Combine role-based and attribute-based access controls for efficient user management.

- Define access based on roles and attributes for streamlined provisioning.
- Automate access changes as users transition roles.

Regularly Audit Resource Access:
Continuously track access needs and remove unnecessary permissions to maintain security.

- Conduct regular audits to prevent over-provisioning.
- Create an auditing schedule to prioritize security.

Centralize Log Collection:
Store logs centrally, preferably in the cloud, ensuring accessibility and compliance without compromising security.

- Stream audit logs to cloud storage or SIEM/SOAR tools for better insights.
- Ensure secure log storage in compliance with cloud IAM practices.

Let's consider for instance IAM Implementation best practices in the manufacturing industry.

In the manufacturing industry, where operational efficiency, intellectual property protection, and supply chain integrity are paramount, implementing a robust Identity and Access Management (IAM) strategy is critical. As manufacturers increasingly adopt digital technologies—such as IoT, industrial control systems (ICS), and cloud-based platforms—securing access to both physical and digital assets become more complex and essential. Effective IAM not only safeguards sensitive data and production systems from cyber threats but also ensures that employees, contractors, and third-party vendors have the appropriate level of access based on their roles and responsibilities. This document outlines best practices for IAM implementation specifically tailored to the unique security and operational demands of the manufacturing sector.

In the manufacturing industry, where operational continuity, intellectual property protection, and supply chain resilience are critical, implementing a robust Identity and Access Management (IAM) framework is no longer optional—it is essential. The rise of Industry 4.0, with its reliance on IoT, smart machines, SCADA systems, and cloud-based platforms, has significantly expanded the threat landscape. As a result, securing access to both digital and physical assets require a strategic, risk-based IAM approach. Effective IAM ensures that employees, contractors, vendors, and even nonhuman entities such as service accounts and industrial sensors have access that is strictly limited to what they need—no more, no less.

Moreover, compliance with regulations and standards such as **NIST SP 800-53**, **IEC 62443**, **ISO/IEC 27001**, and **CMMC** (for defense-related manufacturers) is a driving force behind IAM initiatives. These frameworks emphasize principles like least privilege, separation of duties, and continuous monitoring—core elements of a mature IAM program. By adopting industry-specific best practices in IAM, manufacturers can reduce the risk of cyber incidents, prevent unauthorized access to sensitive data or machinery, and maintain operational efficiency even in highly distributed environments.

This guide outlines proven IAM implementation best practices tailored to the unique security, compliance, and productivity demands of the modern manufacturing landscape.

Introduction of IAM in Cloud Platforms

Identity and Access Management (IAM) is a fundamental security and governance component in all major cloud platforms. It controls **who** can take **what action** on **which resources**, under **what conditions**.

CHAPTER 1   IAM, SECURING IDENTITIES IN THE DIGITALIZATION ERA

The most common IAM cloud planforms are:

- **AWS IAM:**
    - Manages access to AWS services and resources.
    - Uses users, groups, roles, and policies (written in JSON).
    - **Azure Active Directory (AAD):**
        - IAM for Microsoft cloud services (Office 365, Azure).
        - Supports SSO, B2B, B2C, Conditional Access.
- **Google Cloud IAM:**
    - Grants fine-grained access control using roles and policies.

1. **AWS IAM (Identity and Access Management)**
   Key Functions:
    - **Access Management:** Controls access to AWS services and resources.
    - **Entities:** Uses **users**, **groups**, **roles**, and **policies**.
    - **Policies:** Written in **JSON** format and define permissions.

   Details:
    - **Users** are individual accounts (e.g., employees or services).
    - **Groups** let you assign the same policies to multiple users.

CHAPTER 1   IAM, SECURING IDENTITIES IN THE DIGITALIZATION ERA

- **Roles** are assumed by trusted entities (like apps or users from another AWS account).
- **Policies** explicitly allow or deny access to AWS resources.

Example Use Case:

An EC2 instance needs to read data from S3. You assign an IAM **role** to the EC2 instance with a policy that grants s3:GetObject permission.

2. **Azure Active Directory (AAD)**
   Key Functions:

   - IAM system for **Microsoft cloud services** such as **Azure, Office 365**, and Dynamics 365.
   - Supports **Single Sign-On (SSO), Business-to-Business (B2B), Business-to-Consumer (B2C)**, and **Conditional Access**.

   Details:

   - **SSO:** Users log in once to access multiple apps.
   - **B2B:** External users (partners) can access your resources securely.
   - **B2C:** Manages customer identities for applications.
   - **Conditional Access:** Applies access rules based on context like location, device, or user risk.

   Example Use Case:

   You want contractors to log in using their own company's credentials to access your SharePoint Online—this is done via **Azure AD B2B**.

3. **Google Cloud IAM**

   Key Functions:

   - Provides **fine-grained access control** to Google Cloud resources.
   - Uses **roles** and **policies** for defining permissions.

   Details:

   - **Primitive Roles:** Basic predefined roles like Viewer, Editor, Owner.
   - **Predefined Roles:** More granular roles tailored for specific services.
   - **Custom Roles:** Fully tailored roles with specific permissions.
   - IAM policies bind **members** (users, groups, service accounts) to **roles** on **resources**.

   Example Use Case:

   You want to allow a developer access to only deploy functions in **Cloud Functions**, but not to view billing—assign a **custom role** with just the required permissions.

Table 1-1 shows a side-by-side comparison table of AWS IAM, Azure AD, and Google Cloud IAM.

Table 1-1. *Side-by-Side Comparison Table of AWS IAM, Azure AD, and Google Cloud IAM*

Feature/Platform	AWS IAM	Azure Active Directory (AAD)	Google Cloud IAM
Purpose	Access management for AWS resources	Identity management for Microsoft cloud services	Access control for Google Cloud resources
Core Components	Users, Groups, Roles, Policies	Users, Groups, Enterprise Apps, Roles, Conditional Access	Members, Roles, Policies
Policy Language	JSON	JSON-like (via Azure RBAC and Conditional Access rules)	YAML or JSON
Role Types	– Roles for services – Temporary roles	– Directory roles – Azure RBAC roles	– Primitive – Predefined – Custom
Single Sign-On (SSO)	Limited (requires AWS SSO or federated identity)	Built-in SSO across Office 365, Azure, and third-party apps	Supports SSO via Identity Federation
Multi-Factor Auth (MFA)	Supported	Built-in, configurable per user or policy	Supported
B2B/B2C Support	Limited (via IAM Identity Center/Cognito)	Full support: Azure AD B2B & B2C	Via Identity Platform or third-party federation

(continued)

CHAPTER 1   IAM, SECURING IDENTITIES IN THE DIGITALIZATION ERA

Table 1-1. (*continued*)

Feature/ Platform	AWS IAM	Azure Active Directory (AAD)	Google Cloud IAM
Conditional Access	Limited (via SCPs, session policies, ABAC)	Native and highly configurable	Limited (using context-aware access policies)
Custom Roles	JSON policy documents	Custom RBAC roles	Supported
Audit & Logging	CloudTrail	Azure Monitor, AAD Logs	Cloud Audit Logs
Federated Identities	Yes (SAML, OIDC, external IdPs)	Yes (SAML, WS-Fed, OIDC, social logins)	Yes (SAML, OIDC, workload identity federation)
Typical Use Case	Managing fine-grained access to AWS services	Managing access across Office 365, Azure apps, and SaaS	Managing developer and app access to GCP resources

Advanced Insights into Key IAM Features: Industry Applications and Future Trends

As organizations become more digital and interconnected, the importance of sophisticated IAM features—such as Authentication and Authorization, Single Sign-On (SSO), and Multi-Factor Authentication (MFA)—continues to grow. These features are not only crucial for securing sensitive data but also for enabling seamless user experiences. Their implementation varies across industries, shaped by specific regulatory requirements, threat landscapes, and operational needs. Moreover, emerging trends are shaping how these features evolve in the future to meet new challenges.

Industry-Specific Applications include the following:

- **Healthcare:** Compliance with HIPAA and other regulations demands strict access controls. Biometric authentication (like fingerprint or iris scans) is increasingly common for medical staff to securely access electronic health records (EHRs). Role-based access ensures that only authorized personnel—doctors, nurses, or administrators—can view or modify patient data. MFA becomes vital for remote access, especially when healthcare providers need to consult patient data securely from outside the hospital network. For example, telemedicine platforms deploy multi-factor authentication to verify doctors' identities during virtual consultations, ensuring patient privacy.

- **Financial Services:** Security standards such as PCI DSS for payment data, along with regulations like GDPR, necessitate rigorous controls. Banks utilize MFA during online banking, combining passwords with OTPs sent via SMS or authenticator apps. SSO simplifies employee workflows, granting secure, single login access to multiple internal systems, reducing credential management overhead. In trading platforms, real-time risk management requires rapid yet secure access, making adaptive MFA essential to balance user convenience with security demands.

- **Government:** Agencies handle classified information governed by strict security policies. Biometric MFA (fingerprints, retina scans) is commonplace for accessing secure facilities and systems. Federated identity management enables citizens and officials to use a single government-issued credential across multiple agencies, facilitating e-services. These systems often incorporate strict authorization controls based on clearances and roles, with continuous monitoring for insider threats.

- **Retail and E-Commerce:** Customer accounts benefit from SSO integrations with social media platforms, simplifying registration and login processes. MFA during high-value transactions, such as large purchases or changing account details, significantly reduces fraud risks. Retailers increasingly deploy adaptive MFA that analyzes user behavior—like purchase patterns or device fingerprints—to detect anomalies and trigger additional verification steps.

The core security features of IAM—robust Authentication and Authorization, seamless SSO, and multi-layered MFA—are continuously advancing to meet the changing threat landscape and user expectations. Industry-specific deployment, combined with emerging technologies like AI, blockchain, and adaptive security models, will shape the future of IAM. Organizations that stay ahead by adopting these innovations will be better positioned to safeguard their assets, ensure compliance, and deliver frictionless user experiences in an increasingly digital world.

Future Trends in IAM

As digital transformation accelerates across industries, the future of Identity and Access Management (IAM) is evolving to meet new security challenges, regulatory requirements, and user expectations. Traditional IAM models are giving way to more adaptive, intelligent, and decentralized approaches that support hybrid work environments, cloud-native applications, and the growing presence of machine and IoT identities. Emerging technologies such as artificial intelligence (AI), zero trust architecture, and decentralized identity (DID) are reshaping how organizations verify, manage, and secure identities at scale. This section explores the key trends that will define the future of IAM—enabling organizations to build more resilient, user-centric, and risk-aware identity ecosystems.

Here are the most important future trends IAM elements to consider:

- **Zero Trust Security Model:** A central future trend involves moving toward Zero Trust principles, where no user or device is trusted by default. Continuous authentication and dynamic authorization, based on real-time risk assessments, will become standard. This approach relies heavily on adaptive MFA, behavioral analytics, and granular access controls to dynamically evaluate trustworthiness throughout user sessions.

- **Biometric Innovations:** Advances in biometric authentication, including voice recognition, facial recognition, and behavioral biometrics (keystroke dynamics, gait analysis), are expected to provide more seamless yet secure user experiences. These methods reduce friction and increase accuracy in verifying identities, especially in mobile and remote contexts.

- **Decentralized Identity and Blockchain:** Blockchain-based identity management aims to give users control over their digital identities through self-sovereign identities. This approach reduces reliance on centralized identity providers, enhances privacy, and simplifies interoperability across platforms—transforming how Authentication and Authorization are managed globally.

- **Artificial Intelligence and Machine Learning:** AI-driven systems will enhance threat detection and adaptive authentication. By analyzing user behavior and contextual data, these systems will predict and prevent suspicious activities more effectively, allowing for real-time adjustments to MFA requirements and access policies.

- **Passwordless Authentication:** The industry is rapidly shifting toward passwordless solutions, leveraging biometrics, hardware tokens, or cryptographic keys (using standards like WebAuthn). These approaches eliminate weak password vulnerabilities and significantly improve user experience.

Summary

In this chapter, we described why securing digital identities is not merely an operational necessity but a strategic imperative in the digitalization era. It underpins trust, safeguards assets, facilitates compliance, and enables innovation. We explained why IAM and PAM are essential components in building resilient, secure, and trustworthy digital ecosystems.

We introduced in detail IAM and its components like Identification, Authentication, Authorization, Roles, Policies, User Management, etc.

Also we discussed the core security features of IAM such as robust Authentication and Authorization, seamless SSO, and multi-layered MFA.

We defined the IAM from different key industries' perspective like manufacturing and how IAM is used for it. IAM best practices were shortly introduced, and finally we discussed the future of IAM trends like Zero Trust, Biometric, AI, etc.

CHAPTER 2

PAM, Protecting Privileged Accounts and Access Management

In today's digital landscape, where organizations increasingly rely on cloud services, interconnected systems, and remote work, access management has become a cornerstone of cybersecurity and overall operational efficiency. It encompasses the policies, tools, and practices used to control and monitor who can view or use resources within an organization. As technology evolves, so too does the complexity and importance of access management strategies.

In the previous chapter, we described why securing digital identities is not merely an operational necessity but a strategic imperative in the digitalization era. It underpins trust, safeguards assets, facilitates compliance, and enables innovation. We explained why IAM and PAM are essential components in building resilient, secure, and trustworthy digital ecosystems.

We introduced in detail IAM and its components like Identification, Authentication, Authorization, Roles, Policies, User Management, etc.

Also we discussed the core security features of IAM such as robust Authentication and Authorization, seamless SSO, and multi-layered MFA.

In this chapter, we will start first with a deep explanation of Access Management.

Next, we will introduce what is the major difference between a user account and a privileged user account.

What is Zero Trust and why it is so important these days?

We will define what is Zero Trust and why it is so important these days and then introduce and describe PAM (Privileged Access Management) and its components.

Finally, we concentrate on the PAM main differences between IT (Information Technology) and OT (Operational Technology) environments.

The Evolution of Access Management

Historically, access management was straightforward: users were granted permissions based on roles, and authentication tools like passwords were the primary security measure. However, as cyber threats grew sophisticated and organizational structures became more complex, traditional methods proved insufficient. This led to the development of more advanced frameworks like Role-Based Access Control (RBAC), Attribute-Based Access Control (ABAC), and the integration of multi-factor authentication (MFA).

In the modern era, access management is heavily influenced by trends such as cloud computing, mobile device proliferation, and the rising use of APIs and microservices. These developments demand dynamic, scalable, and highly secure access solutions that can adapt quickly to changing requirements.

Key Components of Modern Access Management are as follows:

1. **Identity and Access Management (IAM):**

   Central to modern access management, IAM solutions manage user identities and regulate access across systems. They enable organizations to authenticate users, assign permissions, and enforce policies consistently.

2. **Single Sign-On (SSO):**

   SSO allows users to authenticate once and gain access to multiple applications seamlessly, reducing password fatigue and improving user experience while maintaining security.

3. **Multi-Factor Authentication (MFA):**

   MFA adds layers of security by requiring users to verify their identity through multiple methods, such as a password, a fingerprint, or a one-time code sent to a device.

4. **Zero Trust Architecture:**

   Zero Trust operates on the principle of "never trust, always verify," requiring continuous authentication and verification of user identities and device health before granting access, even within a trusted network.

5. **Access Governance and Auditing:**

   Regular review of permissions, automated access certification, and detailed auditing ensure that only authorized users have access to sensitive resources, aligning with compliance requirements.

CHAPTER 2   PAM, PROTECTING PRIVILEGED ACCOUNTS AND ACCESS MANAGEMENT

Trends Shaping Access Management Today

As organizations increasingly rely on cloud services and remote work, managing who can access what resources is more complex than ever. Emerging trends such as cloud-native solutions, adaptive access control, and biometric authentication are reshaping how access is managed, ensuring that security measures align with modern technological advancements while maintaining flexibility and user convenience.

Here are some of the most important trends shaping the Access Management today:

- **Cloud-Native Solutions:**

    Cloud Identity providers like Azure AD, Okta, and Ping Identity offer scalable, flexible access management that can integrate across diverse cloud services and on-premises systems.

- **Decentralized and Adaptive Access Control:**

    Modern systems adapt user permissions dynamically based on context such as location, device, and behavior patterns, enabling more precise control.

- **Biometric Authentication:**

    Increasingly, biometric modalities like facial recognition and fingerprint scanning are integrated into access workflows for enhanced security.

- **Identity as a Service (IDaaS):**

    Cloud-based identity services simplify deployment, management, and scaling of access control policies across organizations of all sizes.

- **Integration with Business Workflows:**

    Access management now integrates deeply with business processes, enabling automation of provisioning and de-provisioning as roles change.

There are of course also Access Management challenges to consider while modern access management offers numerous benefits. Some of the most important challenges include the following:

- **Balancing Security and User Experience:**

    Overly strict controls can hinder productivity, whereas lax policies can expose organizations to risks.

- **Managing Hidden or Legacy Systems:**

    Older systems may lack compatibility with modern access protocols, requiring additional integration efforts.

- **Ensuring Compliance:**

    Regulations such as GDPR, HIPAA, and ISO standards demand rigorous access controls and auditing.

- **Addressing Insider Threats:**

    Not all threats come from external hackers; insider misuse must be mitigated through monitoring and access controls.

In the realm of cybersecurity, access management is a foundational element that directly impacts an organization's ability to defend against cyber threats. Proper control of who can access what, when, and how can prevent unauthorized intrusions, data breaches, and internal threats. As cyberattacks grow in sophistication, so too must the strategies and tools used to secure access to digital resources.

CHAPTER 2   PAM, PROTECTING PRIVILEGED ACCOUNTS AND ACCESS MANAGEMENT

What Is the Critical Role of Access Management in Cybersecurity?

Cybercriminals often target user accounts, exploiting weak passwords, misconfigured permissions, or compromised devices to infiltrate systems. Effective access management acts as the first line of defense, ensuring that only legitimate users and devices can reach critical assets. It reduces the attack surface and minimizes potential damage from breaches.

Key Cybersecurity Strategies in Modern Access Management include the following:

1. **Identity Verification and Authentication Controls:**

    - Implement Multi-Factor Authentication (MFA): It combines something users know (password), something they have (token or mobile device), or something they are (biometric data). MFA significantly reduces the risk of account compromise.

    - Enforce Strong Password Policies: Use complexity requirements and regular expiration to prevent simple or reused passwords.

2. **Principle of Least Privilege (PoLP):**

    - Restrict users' access rights to only what is necessary for their role. Limiting privileges limits the potential damage from compromised accounts and insider threats.

    - Regularly review and adjust permissions based on role changes or employment status.

3. **Zero Trust Security Model:**
    - It operates on the premise that no user or device should be trusted by default, even inside the network perimeter.
    - Continuously verify user identity and device health before granting access, applying strict controls for sensitive systems.

4. **Continuous Monitoring and Auditing:**
    - Use security information and event management (SIEM) systems to monitor access logs in real-time and detect anomalies.
    - Conduct periodic reviews of access permissions and activity logs to identify suspicious behavior or unauthorized access attempts.

5. **Adaptive and Context-Aware Access Controls:**
    - Employ behavioral analytics to assess risk based on user activity, location, device health, and time.
    - Block or require additional verification for high-risk access attempts, such as unusual location or device.

Challenges Specific to Cybersecurity

- **Phishing and Credential Theft:**

    Attackers often compromise user credentials through sophisticated phishing campaigns, malware, or social engineering. MFA and continuous authentication help mitigate this risk.

- **Insider Threats:**

  Malicious or negligent insiders with excessive permissions can cause significant harm. Enforcing PoLP and conducting regular audits are essential countermeasures.

- **Remote and Cloud Access:**

  The expansion of remote work and cloud services increases exposure points. Zero Trust architectures and VPNs integrated with identity controls are critical.

- **Supply Chain and Third-Party Risks:**

  External partners or vendors with access credentials can become entry points for attackers. Strict third-party access controls and monitoring are necessary.

Emerging Technologies Enhancing Cybersecurity in Access Management

- **Biometric Authentication:**

  Provides a strong, user-friendly verification method, reducing reliance on passwords.

- **Artificial Intelligence and Machine Learning:**

  Enhances anomaly detection and automated response to suspicious activities.

- **Decentralized Identity Systems:**

  Blockchain-based identities could offer tamper-proof, user-controlled access credentials, reducing the risk of centralized breaches.

Best Practices for Cybersecurity-Focused Access Management

- Conduct regular risk assessments to identify vulnerabilities in access controls.

- Implement multi-layered authentication and authorization strategies.

- Integrate access management solutions with broader cybersecurity defenses such as firewalls, intrusion detection systems, and endpoint protection.

- Educate users about cybersecurity best practices, especially regarding credential security and recognizing suspicious activity.

- Develop incident response plans specific to access-related breaches.

The Future of Access Management in Cybersecurity

Looking ahead, access management will become more intelligent and autonomous, leveraging AI and machine learning to detect anomalies and predict potential threats proactively. Federated identity systems and blockchain-based identity verification could further decentralize and secure access processes, enabling seamless and secure interactions across organizational and national boundaries.

Access management in the modern era is a dynamic and critical field that underpins organizational security, compliance, and operational agility. By adopting advanced tools such as IAM, MFA, Zero Trust, and adaptive controls, organizations can protect their assets while providing users with seamless access experiences. As technology continues to evolve, so will the strategies to manage identities and permissions effectively in an increasingly interconnected world.

Core Cybersecurity Strategies to consider in Access Management are as follows:

- **Multi-Factor Authentication (MFA) and Beyond**
- **Principle of Least Privilege (PoLP) with Just-in-Time (JIT) Access**
- **Zero Trust Architecture for Continuous Verification**

We must also understand the emerging trends and future directions like the following:

- **AI-Powered Access Prediction:** Adaptive systems will predict and pre-empt risky access attempts, learning from real-time data.
- **Autonomous Response:** Automated quarantine and access lockdown upon detecting anomalies.
- **Enhanced Identity Verification:** Biometric multimodal verification combining voice, facial recognition, and behavioral biometrics.
- **Federated Identity and Single Sign-On (SSO):** Secure, seamless cross-organizational access, reducing password fatigue and exploiting centralized controls.

From a cybersecurity perspective, access management is vital in safeguarding digital environments against evolving threats. By deploying layered, adaptive, and intelligent access controls, organizations can significantly reduce their vulnerability to cyberattacks, protect sensitive information, and ensure compliance with security standards and regulations. As cyber threats continue to evolve, so must the strategies and technologies dedicated to controlling access in the digital age.

Here are the most important best practices for Cybersecurity-Focused Access Management to consider:

- **Conduct Regular Penetration Testing:** Identify vulnerabilities in identity and access controls.

- **Implement Robust, Multi-Layered Controls:** Combine MFA, PoLP, encryption, and network segmentation.

- **Maintain Comprehensive Audit Trails:** Ensure logs are tamper-proof and enable forensic analysis.

- **Educate Employees:** Continuous cybersecurity awareness training reduces social engineering and credential theft risks.

Cybercriminals deploy tactics such as phishing, malware, credential stuffing, and lateral movement to compromise systems. Once inside, attackers often target privileged accounts, which can lead to catastrophic data exfiltration or system disruption. Effective access management is thus the frontline defense, combining strong identity verification, granular permissions, and continuous monitoring.

Let's introduce now user accounts and privileged accounts.

User Accounts and Privileged Accounts: Key Pillars of Cybersecurity Management

In today's digital landscape, safeguarding enterprise systems hinges significantly on how organizations manage user accounts, especially privileged accounts. While user accounts provide access necessary for daily operations, privileged accounts wield extensive powers that, if misused or compromised, can lead to severe security breaches. Understanding the distinctions, risks, and best practices surrounding these accounts is vital for resilient cybersecurity.

User Accounts Introduction

User accounts serve as the digital identity for employees, contractors, or external partners. They facilitate access to applications and data based on an individual's role and responsibilities. To minimize risks, these accounts are typically granted the minimum permissions needed—adhering to the principle of least privilege.

Example:

A marketing employee may have access to the company's social media platforms and marketing analytics tools but should not have access to financial databases or server configurations. Limiting their permissions reduces the chance of accidental data leaks or malicious activity.

Security measures for User Accounts include the following:

- Strong, unique passwords
- Multi-factor authentication (MFA)
- Regular reviews to revoke unnecessary permissions
- Immediate deactivation upon employee exit or role change

Privileged Accounts Introduction

Privileged accounts, often called admin or superuser accounts, hold superior access rights, allowing control over critical systems, configurations, and sensitive data. These accounts are essential for system administrators, security personnel, and IT support but pose significant security risks if mishandled.

In 2017, the NotPetya cyberattack exploited privileged credentials to spread rapidly across organizations. Attackers used stolen administrator credentials to access Active Directory, enabling widespread entrenchment and data encryption. This incident underscored the devastating impact of compromised privileged accounts.

Typical risks of Privileged Accounts include the following:

- Elevated damage potential for insider threats
- Increased attractiveness for attackers seeking high-value access
- Greater impact if credentials are stolen or misused

Examples of privileged accounts with elevated access rights include (see Figure 2-1) the following:

- **Domain Administrator Accounts:** Have the authority to modify global settings and policies that affect all users, servers, and workstations within a domain.

- **Server Administrator Accounts**: Responsible for managing and maintaining both Windows and Unix/Linux servers.

- **Root or Superuser Accounts**: Found in Unix-like systems, these accounts possess unrestricted read and write access, granting full control over the system.

- **System Administrator Accounts:** Oversee the operation and maintenance of enterprise systems, networks, and computing infrastructure.

- **Local Administrator Accounts**: Have full control over a single machine but no access beyond that specific device.

CHAPTER 2 PAM, PROTECTING PRIVILEGED ACCOUNTS AND ACCESS MANAGEMENT

Figure 2-1. Typical privileged accounts

Let's elaborate the privileged user accounts a bit more.

1. **Domain Administrator Accounts:**

    - **What they are**: High-level accounts in Microsoft Active Directory environments.

    - **Access level**: Full control over domain-wide settings.

    - **Responsibilities**:

        - Managing user accounts and groups.

        - Creating and enforcing Group Policy Objects (GPOs).

        - Configuring domain controllers and authentication policies.

    - **Risks**:

        - If compromised, attackers can take over the entire IT infrastructure.

    - **Typical Use Case**: Enterprise IT teams configuring global security policies.

2. **Server Administrator Accounts:**

    - **What they are**: Accounts with elevated privileges on specific servers (Windows, Unix, or Linux).

- **Access level**: Full administrative access to the server OS.
- **Responsibilities**:
  - Installing and managing server software and services.
  - Performing system updates and patching.
  - Monitoring server performance and logs.
- **Risks**:
  - Can be used to implant malware, backdoors, or alter business-critical services.
- **Typical Use Case**: System administrators maintaining application, file, or database servers.

3. **Root or Superuser Accounts:**
   - **What they are**: The most powerful account in Unix/Linux-based systems.
   - **Access level**: Unrestricted system-wide privileges (read, write, execute).
   - **Responsibilities**:
     - Managing files, services, users, and system configurations.
     - Installing and modifying core OS components.
     - Running scripts or software requiring full access.
   - **Risks**:
     - Root access enables attackers to hide malware, disable logging, or control the entire system.
   - **Typical Use Case**: DevOps teams, IT operations, or software engineers managing Linux servers.

4. **System Administrator Accounts:**

    - **What they are**: Accounts with administrative access across enterprise systems—not always domain-wide.

    - **Access level**: High privileges across selected systems or tools.

    - **Responsibilities**:

        - Maintaining networks, endpoints, storage, and cloud environments.

        - Deploying software, troubleshooting, and ensuring availability.

    - **Risks**:

        - Compromise could allow lateral movement or system-wide misconfigurations.

    - **Typical Use Case**: IT generalists or infrastructure teams managing daily operations.

5. **Local Administrator Accounts:**

    - **What they are**: Admin accounts on a single machine or workstation.

    - **Access level**: Full control but limited to one device.

    - **Responsibilities**:

        - Installing programs, changing settings, and managing users locally.

        - Troubleshooting hardware and software issues.

- **Risks**:
  - Often have weak or reused passwords; targeted in lateral movement attacks.
- **Typical Use Case**: Field technicians, remote workers, or specific legacy systems.

Understanding User Accounts and Privileged Accounts in Cybersecurity

In the realm of cybersecurity, the management of user accounts is fundamental to ensuring organizational security. Among these, privileged accounts hold particular significance due to their extensive access rights, making them prime targets for attackers. Properly understanding and managing both regular user accounts and privileged accounts is critical for protecting digital assets and maintaining a secure IT environment.

User accounts are the digital identities assigned to individuals within an organization. These accounts allow users to access systems, applications, and data necessary for their roles. Regular user accounts typically have restricted permissions, adhering to the principle of least privilege—meaning users only receive access permissions necessary to perform their job functions.

User accounts key points include the following:

- User accounts are essential for accountability and audit trails.
- Proper password policies, multi-factor authentication (MFA), and periodic reviews are vital for securing these accounts.
- Regular users typically have limited permissions to minimize the risk of accidental or malicious damage.

Privileged Accounts: Gatekeepers of Critical Resources

Privileged accounts are special types of user accounts with elevated permissions, allowing the user to access and control sensitive systems, configurations, and data. Examples include administrator accounts, root accounts (in Unix/Linux systems), domain administrators, and service accounts with broad access rights.

Why Are Privileged Accounts Critical?

- They enable essential tasks such as system configuration, software deployment, and security management.
- Because of their extensive access rights, compromised privileged accounts can lead to severe consequences, including data breaches, system outages, and unauthorized data exfiltration.

The very power that privileged accounts hold makes them attractive targets for cybercriminals. Attackers often utilize techniques such as phishing, credential dumping, and privilege escalation to compromise these accounts.

Common risks include the following:

- **Credential theft:** Attackers steal or guess privileged account credentials.
- **Malicious insider activity:** Disgruntled employees or contractors abusing access.
- **Lateral movement:** Using privileged accounts to move across networks and access other sensitive systems.

To mitigate risks, organizations need to implement rigorous management strategies like the following:

1. **Least Privilege Principle:** Grant permissions based on necessity, restricting access for regular users and limiting privileged accounts to essential tasks.

2. **Segregation of Duties:** Separate roles to prevent a single user from having excessive privileges that could be misused.

3. **Regular Audits and Reviews:** Conduct periodic reviews of accounts and permissions to remove or adjust unnecessary privileges.

4. **Multi-Factor Authentication (MFA):** Require MFA for all privileged accounts to add an additional layer of security.

5. **Privileged Access Management (PAM):** Use PAM solutions to control, monitor, and rotate privileged credentials dynamically.

6. **Logging and Monitoring:** Maintain comprehensive logs of account activity to detect suspicious behavior and support incident investigations.

The Importance of Zero Trust in Privileged Account Security

The Zero Trust security model emphasizes verifying every access request, regardless of whether the user is inside or outside the network perimeter. Applying Zero Trust principles to privileged accounts means continuously validating the identity, device health, and context before granting access, reducing the risk of privilege abuse or compromise.

CHAPTER 2   PAM, PROTECTING PRIVILEGED ACCOUNTS AND ACCESS MANAGEMENT

The distinction between regular user accounts and privileged accounts is fundamental in cybersecurity. While user accounts facilitate operations, privileged accounts control critical systems and data, making their security paramount. Organizations must adopt robust practices—such as least privilege, MFA, and PAM—to safeguard these accounts. Implementing comprehensive management strategies not only minimizes the attack surface but also ensures accountability, compliance, and the resilience of IT infrastructure against emerging threats.

What Is Zero Trust?

Zero Trust is a modern cybersecurity framework built on the principle of **"never trust, always verify."** It challenges the outdated assumption that users and devices inside a corporate network are inherently trustworthy. Instead, Zero Trust treats every access request—whether internal or external—as a potential threat until verified.

Originally introduced in 2010 by John Kindervag, then a principal analyst at Forrester Research, Zero Trust has become a foundational approach in protecting today's distributed, hybrid, and cloud-based IT environments.

Traditional security models focus on defending the network perimeter and tend to trust anything inside it. Zero Trust rejects this idea, recognizing that threats can originate from within—whether from compromised devices, insider threats, or stolen credentials.

Zero Trust assumes that attackers may already be inside the network. The goal is to limit their ability to move laterally and minimize potential damage through strict access controls and continuous verification.

The Zero Trust security model challenges traditional perimeter-based defenses by assuming no device or user is trustworthy by default. Applying Zero Trust principles to privileged accounts involves continuous verification, multi-factor access, and dynamic session controls, significantly reducing risk.

CHAPTER 2   PAM, PROTECTING PRIVILEGED ACCOUNTS AND ACCESS MANAGEMENT

Proper management of user and privileged accounts is the cornerstone of a resilient cybersecurity posture. While user accounts are necessary for productivity, privileged accounts warrant extra vigilance due to their high-risk profile. By implementing least privilege policies, leveraging PAM solutions, conducting regular audits, and adopting modern security models like Zero Trust, organizations can substantially reduce their vulnerability to internal and external threats.

The Five Core Principles of Zero Trust

The **Zero Trust** model is grounded in five fundamental pillars that work together to minimize risk, limit exposure, and secure modern digital environments:

1. **Identity Verification:** Trust begins with **proving who or what is requesting access**. Every user, device, and service must be authenticated using strong identity mechanisms, such as **multi-factor authentication (MFA)**, digital certificates, and role-based access controls. No identity is trusted by default—even inside the network.

2. **Application Security:** Applications are secured independently of the network, ensuring that **only authorized and authenticated users** can interact with them. Techniques like **application-layer firewalls**, **runtime protection**, and **whitelisting** are used to enforce secure behavior.

3. **Network Security Segmentation:** The network is divided into **isolated zones** to limit the blast radius of a breach. Each segment enforces its own security policies, and access between segments is tightly controlled. This stops attackers from moving laterally across systems if they gain entry.

4. **Device Security:** Access is contingent on the **security posture of the device**. Devices must meet predefined health and compliance requirements (e.g., up-to-date software, endpoint protection, and encryption). Untrusted or noncompliant devices are denied or restricted.

5. **Data Security/Protection:** Data is classified and protected based on its **sensitivity and criticality**. Encryption is applied both **in transit and at rest**, and access is granted strictly on a **need-to-know basis**. Policies govern who can access what data, under what conditions.

Together, these five pillars form a cohesive **Zero Trust Architecture (ZTA)** that defends against modern threats by assuming breach and verifying continuously.

Figure 2-2 shows the five Core Principles of Zero Trust.

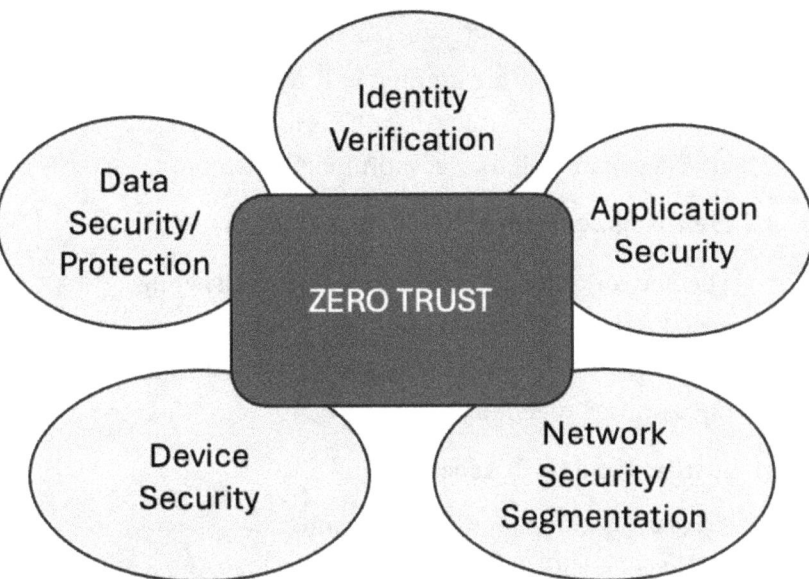

Figure 2-2. *The five core principles of zero trust*

What the Most Common Key Zero Trust Strategies Are?

1. **Segregation of Duties (SoD):**

    No single user or device should have unchecked access to critical systems. Dividing responsibilities helps prevent abuse of power and limits the scope of any compromise. For example:

    - Avoid allowing the same person to both test and deploy code.

    - Prevent self-approved privilege escalations.

2. **Least Privilege Access:**

    Users and devices are granted only the minimum access required for their roles. This limits what attackers can do if they compromise an account.

3. **Microsegmentation:**

    The network is divided into smaller security zones, each with its own access controls. This prevents attackers from freely navigating across systems if one zone is breached.

4. **Just-in-Time (JIT) Access:**

    Access is granted temporarily—only when needed—and revoked automatically after use. This reduces the risk of persistent credentials being exploited.

5. **Multifactor Authentication (MFA):**

    MFA ensures that a password alone isn't enough to gain access. A second verification step—such as a one-time code sent to a user's phone—is required.

6. **Auditing and Session Tracking:**

    All activity is logged, and privileged sessions are recorded. This provides a reliable audit trail for investigations and compliance and helps feed alerts to SIEM systems.

How Zero Trust Works?

Here are the common steps about how Zero Trust works.

1. **Authenticate Everything:**

   Every access request is verified using strong authentication methods like **multi-factor authentication (MFA)** and device validation. Trust is established continuously—not just at login.

2. **Enforce Least Privilege:**

   Users, applications, and devices are granted **only the access necessary** to perform their specific roles. This limits exposure if credentials or endpoints are compromised.

3. **Continuously Monitor and Analyze:**

   Zero Trust environments employ **real-time monitoring and behavioral analytics** to detect unusual activity and potential threats. Every access event is logged and assessed.

4. **Micro-Segment the Network:**

   The network is broken into **isolated zones** to prevent lateral movement. If an attacker gains access to one segment, they can't automatically move to others.

5. **Apply Context-Aware Access Controls:**

   Access decisions factor in **contextual data** such as user identity, device health, geolocation, time of access, and data sensitivity. Policies adjust dynamically based on this context.

6. **Automate Detection and Response:**

   Threats are met with **automated, policy-driven responses**, reducing response time and limiting impact. Orchestration tools ensure consistent enforcement across systems and platforms.

Let's introduce PAM now.

What Is Privileged Access Management (PAM)?

Privileged Access Management (PAM) is a critical cybersecurity discipline that focuses on controlling, securing, monitoring, and auditing access to systems and data by privileged users—both human and non-human (e.g., applications, scripts, or automated tools). PAM is a subset of **Identity and Access Management (IAM)** and is vital for reducing the risks associated with credential theft, privilege misuse, and unauthorized access to sensitive systems.

The components of PAM are shown in Figure 2-3.

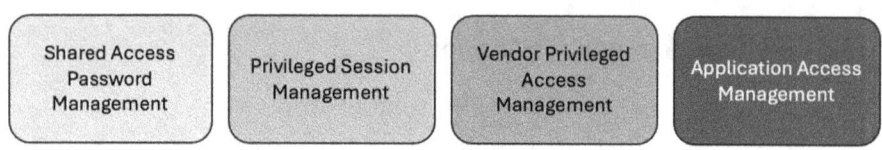

Figure 2-3. Components of PAM

PAM is often associated with related terms like **Privileged Identity Management (PIM)** or **Privileged Access Security (PAS)**. It is fundamentally based on the **principle of least privilege**, which ensures users are granted only the access necessary to perform their job duties. This approach reduces the attack surface and helps prevent insider threats and external attacks.

CHAPTER 2   PAM, PROTECTING PRIVILEGED ACCOUNTS AND ACCESS MANAGEMENT

Understanding Privileged Access:

Privileged access refers to elevated rights or permissions that go beyond those granted to standard users. These permissions allow users to manage, configure, and maintain IT infrastructure and critical systems. Examples include the following:

- **Root Access**: Full control over a system, including unrestricted ability to alter configurations or delete files.

- **Administrator Access:** Permission to manage operating systems, software, and user accounts.

- **Service Account Access:** Noninteractive accounts used by systems and applications to perform automated tasks.

Any account with command-line access, elevated permissions, or control over critical infrastructure—such as CRM systems, network switches, or industrial control systems (ICS)—may be considered privileged.

Privileged Accounts vs. Privileged Access

- **Privileged Accounts** are user profiles with elevated permissions (e.g., sysadmins, network engineers).

- **Privileged Access** is the actual capability granted to these accounts to perform sensitive operations.

These accounts are primary targets for cyberattacks due to the valuable systems and data they can access. Effective PAM ensures these accounts are tightly controlled and monitored.

Traditional PAM: Core Functions and Tools

Traditional PAM solutions focus on several key capabilities:

- **Password Vaulting:** Storing and rotating passwords for shared accounts.

- **Session Monitoring:** Recording and tracking privileged user actions.

- **Access Control:** Granting access based on policy, role, or approval workflow.

- **Command Filtering:** Restricting allowed actions during privileged sessions.

- **Dual Control (Four-Eyes Principle):** Requiring multiple users to approve or supervise access.

- **Integration:** Connecting with IT service management (ITSM), ticketing, and change management systems.

- **Credential Management:** Managing SSH keys, API tokens, and other sensitive credentials.

These systems typically secure access to a wide range of infrastructure including operating systems, applications, hypervisors, network devices, IoT, and SaaS platforms.

Key Functional Categories in PAM

1. **Shared Account Password Management (SAPM):**

   It manages shared credentials, supports password rotation and approval workflows, and integrates with ITSM systems. Vaults often support other secrets like SSH keys, though typically with limited lifecycle management capabilities.

CHAPTER 2 PAM, PROTECTING PRIVILEGED ACCOUNTS AND ACCESS MANAGEMENT

2. **Superuser Privilege Management (SUPM):**

   It controls and audits use of root or administrator privileges. Implements just-in-time access, restricts scope (least privilege), and monitors elevated activity.

3. **Application-to-Application Password Management (AAPM):**

   It enables applications and scripts to securely retrieve credentials from vaults instead of storing them in code, though this carries its own risks if improperly secured.

4. **Privilege Elevation and Delegation Management (PEDM):**

   It grants users elevated access dynamically and with granularity, limiting access duration and scope.

5. **Privileged Session Management (PSM):**

   It initiates, monitors, and records privileged sessions. It may support SSO or MFA for access and integrate with SIEM tools.

6. **Privileged Account and Session Management (PASM):**

   It combines credential management and session monitoring to protect privileged accounts and their usage end-to-end.

CHAPTER 2   PAM, PROTECTING PRIVILEGED ACCOUNTS AND ACCESS MANAGEMENT

Privileged Credential Management

Privileged credentials include the following:

- **Passwords**
- **SSH Keys**
- **API Tokens**

These credentials provide elevated access to sensitive systems and must be secured through methods such as password vaulting, encryption, rotation, and multi-factor authentication (MFA).

Why PAM Is Important?

PAM is vital due to the following reasons:

- **Security Threats:** Privileged accounts are frequent targets for cyberattacks.
- **Insider Risk:** Privileged users (e.g., system admins, developers) have potential for misuse.
- **Compliance:** Regulatory requirements often mandate strict control over privileged access.
- **Operational Efficiency:** PAM reduces human error and improves access governance.
- **Vendor Risk:** External contractors or third parties often require elevated access and must be managed securely.

PAM vs. PIM

- **Privileged Access Management (PAM):**

    Encompasses tools and practices for managing and auditing privileged access across IT systems.

- **Privileged Identity Management (PIM):**

    Focuses on managing the identities tied to privileged roles, ensuring only authorized users can assume them.

Together, PAM and PIM provide a more comprehensive security solution—PIM ensures the right identities get access, and PAM governs what they can do once access is granted.

PAM vs. IAM

- **Identity and Access Management (IAM):**

    Manages user identities and access across an organization. Covers standard users and general access needs.

- **Privileged Access Management (PAM):**

    Specializes in high-risk, high-privilege access, adding stricter controls and oversight for elevated accounts.

IAM sets the baseline for identity and access, while PAM builds upon it to secure sensitive environments more thoroughly.

PAM and the Principle of Least Privilege

PAM operationalizes **least privilege** by

- Restricting elevated access to what's necessary.
- Granting access only when needed (just-in-time).
- Revoking access automatically after use.
- Monitoring and auditing all privileged actions.

This alignment significantly reduces the risk of misuse or compromise of powerful accounts.

Challenges with Traditional PAM in the Cloud

Traditional PAM systems face limitations in modern cloud and containerized environments:

- **Complex Deployments:** Setup can be time-consuming and disruptive to administrator workflows.
- **Scalability Issues:** Password vaults and jump servers don't scale well in dynamic, elastic environments.
- **Automation Friction:** Scripts and services must be rewritten to pull credentials from vaults.
- **Single Points of Failure:** Centralized vaults create new vulnerabilities.
- **Poor Fit for Cloud:** Cloud-native environments require faster, more flexible access models.

Modern PAM must evolve beyond traditional vaulting to address these limitations.

CHAPTER 2   PAM, PROTECTING PRIVILEGED ACCOUNTS AND ACCESS MANAGEMENT

Privileged Access Management (PAM) is essential for securing an organization's most sensitive assets. By enforcing least privilege, monitoring high-level access, and securing credentials, PAM reduces the risk of breaches and supports compliance. As IT environments evolve—especially with the rise of cloud and automation—PAM strategies must also advance to meet new challenges efficiently and securely.

Let's understand now the key differences in IT (Information Technology) vs OT (Operational Technology) PAM.

Key Differences Between IT and OT Privileged Access Management (PAM)

Privileged Access Management (PAM) plays a crucial role in both IT (Information Technology) and OT (Operational Technology) environments, but the approaches and priorities differ significantly due to the nature of the systems involved.

IT PAM focuses on securing data centers, cloud infrastructure, servers, applications, and network devices. The primary goal is to protect sensitive data and maintain system integrity while enabling flexible access for administrators and developers. IT environments often use technologies like SSH, RDP, VPN, and APIs to manage privileged access. Security measures emphasize confidentiality, compliance, and operational efficiency, with features like role-based access control, just-in-time access, multi-factor authentication, and detailed session monitoring.

In contrast, **OT PAM** secures industrial control systems such as SCADA, PLCs, sensors, and other devices that manage critical physical processes in industries like manufacturing, energy, and utilities. OT systems often involve legacy equipment with proprietary protocols and have strict operational constraints because downtime can cause safety hazards, production loss, or physical damage. Access methods in OT may include serial connections and specialized industrial protocols, with some use of SSH on modern Linux-based devices. OT PAM focuses heavily on availability, safety, and reliability, often requiring more static and controlled access with emergency override capabilities. Monitoring and auditing can be more challenging due to legacy system limitations, but increasing adoption of PAM solutions is helping improve visibility.

While **IT PAM** deals with dynamic, frequently changing environments, **OT PAM** must prioritize stable and continuous operation. Compliance requirements also vary: IT PAM aligns with standards like GDPR, HIPAA, and PCI-DSS, whereas OT PAM adheres to industrial and safety-specific standards such as IEC 62443 and NERC CIP.

In summary, IT and OT PAM share the goal of protecting privileged access but differ in environments, risks, technologies, and operational priorities. Understanding these differences is essential for implementing effective PAM solutions tailored to each domain.

More simply

- **IT PAM** focuses on securing dynamic, highly interconnected systems with frequent updates and flexible access needs.

- **OT PAM** must balance security with operational continuity, handling legacy devices and strict uptime requirements in industrial environments.

Table 2-1 shows the key differences in IT vs OT PAM.

Table 2-1. *Key Differences in IT vs. OT PAM*

Aspect	IT PAM	OT PAM
Primary Environment	Data centers, cloud, servers, workstations, network infrastructure	Industrial control systems (ICS), SCADA, PLCs, DCS, OT networks
Types of Assets Managed	Servers, databases, cloud instances, applications, network devices	Industrial controllers, sensors, actuators, proprietary devices, legacy systems
Access Methods	SSH, RDP, VPN, APIs, GUI-based admin tools	Serial connections, specialized industrial protocols, some SSH for Linux-based devices
Operational Constraints	Typically flexible, with scheduled maintenance windows	Highly sensitive, often 24/7 operations with zero tolerance for downtime or disruption
Security Priorities	Confidentiality, integrity, availability, compliance	Safety, availability, real-time reliability, and preventing operational disruption
User Base	System admins, developers, DBAs, cloud engineers	Control engineers, plant operators, vendors, sometimes less IT-savvy personnel
Risk Factors	Data breaches, ransomware, insider threats	Physical damage, safety incidents, production downtime, sabotage

(*continued*)

CHAPTER 2   PAM, PROTECTING PRIVILEGED ACCOUNTS AND ACCESS MANAGEMENT

Table 2-1. (*continued*)

Aspect	IT PAM	OT PAM
Privileged Accounts	Admin accounts, root users, service accounts, API keys, SSH keys	Control system admin accounts, device-level accounts, vendor access accounts
Access Controls	Role-based access control (RBAC), just-in-time access, multi-factor authentication	Often more static due to operational stability, sometimes manual controls, emergency access needed
Monitoring and Auditing	Detailed session recording, command filtering, automated alerts	Often limited due to legacy systems, but increasing adoption of session monitoring and anomaly detection
Integration with Other Systems	SIEM, Identity Governance, Cloud platforms	OT asset management, safety systems, network monitoring
Technology Challenges	Dynamic cloud environments, hybrid IT, automation	Legacy devices, proprietary protocols, limited software patching, physical security concerns
Compliance Standards	GDPR, HIPAA, PCI-DSS, SOX, NIST	NERC CIP, IEC 62443, NIST SP 800-82, industry-specific safety standards

Most Common PAM Vendors for IT Environments

Let's see the list of the most common PAM for IT vendors:

1. **SSH**

    - **Secure and control remote SSH access** to critical systems, reducing unauthorized entry risks.

    - **Centralize SSH key management** with automated rotation and lifecycle controls to prevent key misuse.

    - **Monitor and record SSH sessions** for auditing, compliance, and insider threat detection.

    - **Enforce least privilege access** and multi-factor authentication for stronger security.

    - **Support both IT and OT environments**, protecting diverse systems that use SSH.

2. **CyberArk**

    - Industry leader in IT PAM.

    - Comprehensive password vault, session management, and SSH key management.

    - Widely deployed in enterprises globally.

3. **BeyondTrust**

    - Strong IT PAM with endpoint privilege management.

    - Integrates well with IT infrastructure and supports session monitoring.

4. **Delinea (Thycotic+Centrify)**
   - Popular for IT PAM and cloud environments.
   - Offers Secret Server and Privilege Cloud solutions.
5. **One Identity**
   - Integrated identity and privileged access management.
   - Supports broad IT environments.
6. **ManageEngine PAM360**
   - Cost-effective option for IT PAM.
   - Password and session management with SSH key support.
7. **HashiCorp Vault**
   - For DevOps and cloud-native IT infrastructure.
   - Focused on secrets management and dynamic credential generation.

Most Common PAM Vendors for OT Environments

OT environments (like manufacturing, energy, utilities) have unique PAM needs due to critical infrastructure, legacy systems, and real-time operations:

1. **SSH**
   - **Secure remote access** to critical operational technology systems via SSH.
   - **Manage and rotate SSH keys** to prevent unauthorized access and reduce risks from stale credentials.

CHAPTER 2   PAM, PROTECTING PRIVILEGED ACCOUNTS AND ACCESS MANAGEMENT

- **Monitor SSH sessions** for visibility into user actions on sensitive OT devices.
- **Enforce strict access controls** and least privilege principles tailored for OT environments.

2. **CyberArk**
   - Offers OT-specific PAM solutions.
   - Supports critical infrastructure and industrial control systems (ICS).
   - Provides secure access to SCADA, PLCs, and other OT assets.

3. **BeyondTrust**
   - Delivers PAM adapted to OT environments.
   - Can secure privileged access to ICS, SCADA, and network devices.

4. **Tenable (formerly Indegy)**
   - Focuses on OT security and asset management.
   - Integrates with PAM to monitor privileged access in OT networks.

5. **Nozomi Networks**
   - OT/IoT security platform.
   - Works alongside PAM solutions to monitor privileged user activity.

6. **Wallix**
   - Offers PAM for IT and OT.
   - Designed for complex environments including critical infrastructure.

7. **Centrify (now part of Delinea)**
   - Provides PAM capabilities that extend into OT with secure remote access features.

Figure 2-4 shows a comparison of PAM capabilities IT/OT Vendors.

	SSH	BeyondTrust	Wallix	Claroty	Cyolo	Xage
Account and asset discovery	●	●	◐	○	○	○
Secure remote access	●	●	●	●	●	●
Passwordless	●	○	○	○	○	○
File and data transfer security	●	●	●	●	●	●
Fine-grained access control	●	●	●	◐	◐	◐
SSH key management	●	◐	◐	○	○	○
Quantum-safe	●	○	○	○	○	○
Auditing and monitoring	●	●	●	●	●	●

***Figure 2-4.** Comparison of PAM capabilities of IT/OT Vendors*

Summary

In this chapter, we started with a deep explanation of Access Management starting with the evolution of it and how as cyber threats grew sophisticated and organizational structures became more complex, traditional methods proved insufficient and why this has led to the development of more advanced frameworks like Role-Based Access Control (RBAC), Attribute-Based Access Control (ABAC), and the integration of multi-factor authentication (MFA).

We then explained a bit about the key components of modern Access Management in the cybersecurity perspective.

Next, we introduced what the major differences between a user account and a privileged user account are.

CHAPTER 2   PAM, PROTECTING PRIVILEGED ACCOUNTS AND ACCESS MANAGEMENT

We defined what is Zero Trust and why it is so important these days and then introduced and described PAM (Privileged Access Management) and its components.

Finally, we concentrated on the PAM main differences between IT (Information Technology) and OT (Operational Technology) environments.

CHAPTER 3

IAM and PAM Risks, Impacts, and Challenges

In our modern digital era, organizations increasingly rely on Identity and Access Management (IAM) and Privileged Access Management (PAM) to secure their systems, data, and operational environments. While these technologies are crucial for reducing security risks, they also introduce their own set of vulnerabilities, operational challenges, and potential impacts if not properly managed. Understanding these risks, impacts, and challenges is essential for cybersecurity professionals striving to safeguard organizational assets effectively.

In the previous chapter, we provided a deep explanation of Access Management.

We introduced what is the major difference between a user account and a privileged user account.

We defined what is Zero Trust and why it is so important these days and then introduced and described PAM (Privileged Access Management) and its components.

Finally, we concentrated on the PAM main differences between IT (Information Technology) and OT (Operational Technology) environments.

CHAPTER 3   IAM AND PAM RISKS, IMPACTS, AND CHALLENGES

Now it's time to discuss IAM and PAM cybersecurity major risks, impacts, and challenges.

The most common **Identity and Access Management (IAM)** and **Privileged Access Management (PAM)** risks revolve around the following:

- **Misconfigurations**
- **Lack of visibility**
- **Overprovisioning**
- **Weak controls**

In general, the most common IAM risks include the following:

- **Overprovisioned Access (Excessive Privileges):**
  - Users have more access than necessary, increasing the attack surface.
  - Violates the principle of least privilege.
- **Stale or Orphaned Accounts:**
  - Accounts that belong to former employees or unused service accounts.
  - These can be hijacked and used maliciously.
- **Poor Credential Hygiene:**
  - Weak, reused, or shared passwords.
  - Lack of MFA (multi-factor authentication).
- **Inadequate Role-Based Access Controls (RBAC):**
  - Inconsistent role definitions lead to access creep and entitlement sprawl.

- **Lack of Identity Federation and SSO Control:**
  - Improper integration with federated identity providers or misconfigured SSO leads to authentication loopholes.
- **Shadow IT and Unauthorized Access:**
  - Use of unsanctioned tools and apps bypasses IAM controls.
- **Insufficient Logging and Monitoring:**
  - Inability to detect or respond to suspicious access activities in real-time.

Here are the most **common PAM risks:**

1. **Shared or Hardcoded Privileged Credentials**
   - Common in scripts or legacy apps—easy to leak and hard to rotate.
2. **No Session Recording or Auditing**
   - Lack of traceability makes it difficult to investigate incidents or enforce accountability.
3. **Privileged Access via VPN or Direct Access**
   - Bypasses PAM tools, giving users direct, unmonitored access to critical systems.
4. **Standing Privileges (Always-On Admin Rights)**
   - Persistent elevated access increases exposure in case of credential theft.
5. **Credential Vault Mismanagement**
   - Insecure or poorly integrated vaulting solutions expose secrets to unauthorized users.

6. **Third-Party Vendor Access Risks**
   - External users may be granted overprivileged or unrestricted access without session controls.

7. **Weak Integration with IAM Systems**
   - PAM not linked with IAM leads to mismatched policies and fragmented control.

In general, for both IAM and PAM, we must apply the following mitigation best practices:

- Enforce **least privilege** and **just-in-time access**.
- Automate **provisioning/deprovisioning** and **access reviews**.
- Use **MFA everywhere**, especially for privileged accounts.
- Implement **session recording**, **vaulting**, and **audit trails**.
- Continuously monitor for **anomalies** and **access abuse**.

Let's expand these best practices a bit more:

1. **Enforce Least Privilege and Just-In-Time Access:**
   a. Ensure users and administrators are granted only the permissions necessary to perform their specific roles and tasks.
   b. Implement just-in-time (JIT) access to provide temporary elevated privileges only when needed, reducing the attack surface.

c. Regularly review permissions to prevent privilege creep and ensure compliance with security policies.

2. **Automate Provisioning, Deprovisioning, and Access Reviews:**

    a. Use automation tools to streamline the onboarding and offboarding processes, ensuring timely revocation of access for departing users.

    b. Schedule periodic access reviews and audits to validate that only authorized users retain the appropriate access rights.

    c. Reduce human error and improve efficiency by avoiding manual, error-prone processes.

3. **Use Multi-Factor Authentication (MFA) Everywhere, Especially for Privileged Accounts:**

    a. Implement MFA across all access points to significantly reduce the risk of credential theft or misuse.

    b. Place extra emphasis on securing privileged accounts with additional authentication layers, such as hardware tokens or biometric verification.

    c. Ensure MFA is consistently applied to remote, administrative, and sensitive access scenarios.

4. **Implement Session Recording, Vaulting, and Audit Trails:**

    a. Record user sessions, particularly those involving privileged accounts, to enable detailed audits and troubleshooting.

    b. Store sensitive credentials and secrets securely in vaults with strict access controls.

    c. Maintain comprehensive audit logs that document access events, actions taken, and any anomalies for accountability and forensic analysis.

5. **Continuously Monitor for Anomalies and Access Abuse:**

    a. Utilize security information and event management (SIEM) systems and behavioral analytics to detect unusual activities in real-time.

    b. Set up alerts for suspicious behaviors, such as abnormal login times, locations, or actions.

    c. Respond swiftly to potential security incidents to prevent or mitigate damage.

By following these best practices, organizations can significantly strengthen their IAM and PAM frameworks, reduce vulnerabilities, and ensure regulatory compliance.

Risks, Impacts, and Operational Challenges Associated with IAM and PAM in Modern Cybersecurity

In today's digital landscape, organizations are heavily reliant on Identity and Access Management (IAM) and Privileged Access Management (PAM) to secure critical systems, safeguard sensitive data, and ensure operational resilience. While these technologies are powerful tools in defending against cyber threats, they also carry inherent risks and operational challenges. Understanding these risks—along with their impacts and mitigation strategies—is vital for cybersecurity professionals and organizations committed to maintaining a strong security posture.

While IAM and PAM are essential components of modern cybersecurity strategies, they come with inherent risks, impacts, and operational challenges. Effective management of these risks requires a well-thought-out strategy, ongoing monitoring, and a culture of security awareness. By understanding and addressing these challenges proactively, organizations can significantly reduce their attack surface, ensure compliance, and maintain operational resilience in an increasingly threat-prone environment.

Please remember that ineffective or poorly managed IAM and PAM pose serious risks that can impact organizations across technical, financial, regulatory, and reputational dimensions—emphasizing the necessity of robust, properly governed identity and privilege controls.

The most common IAM (Identity and Access Management) and PAM (Privileged Access Management) cybersecurity risks include the following:

1. **Credential Theft and Compromise:** Attackers often target user credentials, especially privileged accounts, through phishing, malware, or credential stuffing, gaining unauthorized access.

2. **Misconfiguration of Access Controls:** Incorrect permissions, overly broad roles, or failure to revoke access can expose sensitive data or systems unnecessarily.

3. **Weak Authentication Methods:** Use of weak passwords or absence of multi-factor authentication (MFA) makes it easier for attackers to impersonate users and escalate privileges.

4. **Stale or Excess Privileged Accounts:** Leaving privileged accounts active after an employee leaves or after roles change increases the attack surface.

5. **Lack of Proper Session Monitoring:** Inadequate activity logging and session recording make it difficult to detect malicious or unauthorized activities, allowing breaches to go unnoticed.

6. **Insufficient Privilege Enforcement:** Failure to enforce least privilege principles can lead to users having more access than necessary, escalating risks of insider threats or accidental damage.

7. **Inadequate Lifecycle Management:** Poor onboarding, role changes, and de-provisioning processes can leave outdated or unnecessary access in place.

8. **Lack of Segmentation and Segregation of Duties:** Insufficient network or system segmentation can allow attackers to move laterally, especially if privileged accounts are not properly isolated.

9. **Over-Reliance on Single Security Measures:**
   Relying solely on passwords without MFA or session monitoring leaves gaps that attackers can exploit.

10. **Insufficient Education and Awareness:** Users may fall victim to phishing or social engineering, leading to credential compromise or privilege misuse.

These cybersecurity risks highlight the importance of strong policies, automation, regular audits, and layered security controls to mitigate potential vulnerabilities in IAM and PAM systems.

What Are the Most Common IAM and PAM Cybersecurity Impacts?

The most common impacts of weaknesses or failures in IAM (Identity and Access Management) and PAM (Privileged Access Management) include the following:

1. **Data Breaches and Information Loss:**
   Unauthorized access due to compromised credentials or misconfigured permissions can lead to extensive data theft or exposure of sensitive information, damaging trust and incurring regulatory penalties.

2. **Operational Disruption:** Attackers gaining control over critical systems—especially in industrial, financial, or healthcare environments—can cause system outages, safety hazards, or process interruptions, leading to financial losses and safety risks.

3. **Financial Losses:** Breaches and operational disruptions can result in significant costs: legal penalties, remediation expenses, downtime, lost revenue, and increased cybersecurity insurance premiums.

4. **Regulatory Non-Compliance:** Failing to properly manage identities and privileges can lead to violations of regulations such as GDPR, HIPAA, PCI DSS, or industry-specific standards, with hefty fines and legal consequences.

5. **Reputational Damage:** Publicized security breaches involving privilege misuse or unauthorized access erode customer and stakeholder trust, often resulting in long-term brand damage.

6. **Loss of Intellectual Property:** Privilege abuse or cyber-espionage can lead to theft of trade secrets, research data, or proprietary information, which can harm competitiveness and innovation.

7. **Increased Insider Threats:** Weak IAM/PAM controls increase the risk of insider threats, whether malicious or accidental, with potentially devastating impacts on the organization.

8. **Legal and Litigation Risks:** Data breaches or unauthorized disclosures can lead to legal actions from customers, partners, or regulators, increasing financial and reputational burden.

Let's explain a bit more about the most common cybersecurity risks associated with IAM and PAM.

- **Misconfiguration and Human Error:** Many security breaches originate from misconfigured IAM and PAM controls—such as overly broad permissions, incorrect role assignments, or failure to revoke access promptly. Human errors during setup or maintenance can inadvertently expose critical systems or privileged accounts. The following points are to be considered:

  - **Elaboration:**

    Misconfigured access controls are among the most common root causes of security breaches. For example, misconfigured IAM permissions on cloud platforms like AWS or Azure can leave critical resources open to the public. In one notable case, a misconfigured S3 bucket exposed millions of private customer records, leading to a data leak.

  - **Best Practice:**

    Regularly audit IAM policies and permissions, use principle of least privilege, and adopt automated tools that flag over-permissioned or unused accounts.

- **Credential Theft and Stolen Identities:** Attackers target IAM systems to steal credentials, especially privileged accounts, using phishing, malware, or credential stuffing. Once compromised, attackers can move laterally across networks, access sensitive data, or disrupt operations. The following points are to be considered:

- **Elaboration:**

  Attackers target privileged accounts because they provide extensive access. In the infamous SolarWinds breach, attackers used stolen credentials to infiltrate numerous organizations. Phishing campaigns and credential stuffing are common attack methods that can compromise these high-value accounts.

- **Best Practice:**

  Employ multi-factor authentication (MFA), enforce strong password policies, and monitor for signs of credential compromise using anomaly detection tools.

• **Insufficient Multi-Factor Authentication (MFA):** Lack of MFA or weak authentication mechanisms for IAM and privileged accounts can allow attackers to bypass security controls, gaining unauthorized access and escalating privileges. The following points are to be considered:

- **Elaboration:**

  Weak passwords are the easiest attack vector. Many breaches exploit default or easily guessable admin passwords. For example, in 2020, hackers accessed a US government contractor's network due to weak passwords on administrator accounts.

- **Best Practice:**

  Implement MFA across all privileged and sensitive access points and adopt password vaulting solutions that enforce complex password policies.

CHAPTER 3   IAM AND PAM RISKS, IMPACTS, AND CHALLENGES

- **Inadequate Privileged Session Monitoring:** Without proper session monitoring and recording, malicious or accidental activities carried out by privileged users may go undetected, making incident response difficult. The following points are to be considered:

  - **Elaboration:**

    Without proper session monitoring, malicious activities—like privilege escalation or unauthorized data access—can go unnoticed. For instance, in the 2018 Facebook incident, misused privileged privileges were only detected long after harm occurred due to inadequate activity logs.

  - **Best Practice:**

    Use privileged session recording and real-time activity monitoring to detect suspicious actions early. Security Information and Event Management (SIEM) tools help aggregate and analyze these logs.

- **Inadequate Lifecycle Management:** Failure to promptly revoke or modify access when employees leave, change roles, or when systems are decommissioned can leave stale or high-risk accounts active, increasing threat exposure. The following points are to be considered:

  - **Elaboration:**

    Accounts of former employees or contractors sometimes remain active for months or years, providing an entry point for attackers. For example, in a notable case, an insider used an abandoned account to access sensitive data over a long period.

- **Best Practice:**

  Automate account deprovisioning workflows, perform regular access reviews, and immediately revoke permissions when employment ends or roles change.

Impacts of IAM and PAM failures include the following:

- **Data Breaches and Data Loss:** Compromised identities, especially in privileged accounts, can lead to significant data breaches, exposing sensitive customer, financial, or intellectual property data. The following points are to be considered:

  - **Elaboration:**

    Stolen privileged credentials enable attackers to extract sensitive or proprietary data, leading to severe financial and reputational consequences. A breach at Target in 2013 involved stolen credentials leading to data compromise of millions of customers.

- **Operational Disruption:** Unauthorized or malicious access can cause system outages, manipulation of industrial control systems in manufacturing, or disruption of critical services, resulting in costly downtime or safety hazards. The following points are to be considered:

  - **Elaboration:**

    In sectors like manufacturing or critical infrastructure, compromised privileged accounts can disable control systems or disrupt supply chains. For example, a cyberattack on a hospital's network using compromised admin credentials caused patient record disruptions.

- **Regulatory Non-Compliance:** Failure to enforce proper IAM and PAM controls can result in violations of regulations such as GDPR, HIPAA, or NIST standards, leading to hefty fines and legal repercussions. The following points are to be considered:

  - **Elaboration:**

    Inadequate access controls can lead to GDPR or HIPAA violations, resulting in fines. For instance, a healthcare entity failed to secure access to patient records, leading to costly penalties.

- **Reputational Damage:** Security incidents involving identity breaches diminish customer trust and damage brand reputation, sometimes with long-lasting effects. The following points are to be considered:

  - **Elaboration:**

    A breach involving privilege misuse often erodes trust among customers, partners, and regulators. After a major breach, the affected company's stock value often drops, and customer loyalty diminishes.

- **Financial Loss:** The cost of incident response, legal liabilities, remediation efforts, and potential regulatory fines can be substantial, impacting organizational profitability. The following points are to be considered:

  - **Elaboration:**

    Remediation costs, legal penalties, and downtime expenses can mount quickly. For example, the NotPetya malware caused billions in damages partly owing to vulnerabilities in privileged account controls.

CHAPTER 3 IAM AND PAM RISKS, IMPACTS, AND CHALLENGES

What Was the NotPetya Malware Attack?

The NotPetya attack was a sophisticated and destructive cyber incident that exploited existing vulnerabilities to spread rapidly, primarily disrupting Ukrainian institutions and causing global operational chaos. Its primary objective was likely geopolitical, aimed at destabilization rather than financial gain.

The NotPetya malware attack was a highly destructive cyberattack that occurred in June 2017, primarily targeting organizations in Ukraine but also affecting companies worldwide. It is widely considered one of the most damaging ransomware incidents, though its true intent and nature go beyond typical ransomware operations.

Key Details:

- **Origin and Attribution:** NotPetya is believed to have been a state-sponsored cyberattack, most likely attributed to Russian interests, although the exact perpetrators have not been officially confirmed.

- **Mechanism and Spread:** The malware initially propagated through a compromised update mechanism of a popular Ukrainian accounting software called M.E.Doc. It then spread rapidly across networks using exploiting vulnerabilities like the EternalBlue exploit (also used in WannaCry) and other lateral movement techniques.

- **Nature of the Malware:** Although it displayed characteristics similar to ransomware—such as encrypting files and demanding payment—the primary goal appeared to be widespread disruption and destruction of data. The malware irreversibly encrypted critical system files, effectively crippling affected organizations' IT infrastructure.

CHAPTER 3   IAM AND PAM RISKS, IMPACTS, AND CHALLENGES

- **Impact:**

  - Major Ukrainian government agencies, banks, and energy companies were severely affected.

  - Several international firms, including shipping giant Maersk, pharmaceutical company Merck, and others, experienced operational disruptions, financial losses, and data loss.

  - It caused an estimated $10 billion in damages worldwide.

- **Unique Aspects:** Unlike typical ransomware that seeks monetary ransom payments, NotPetya caused irreversible data destruction and was considered a cyberweapon aimed at destabilizing targets, especially in Ukraine.

What Are the Most Common IAM and PAM Challenges?

The most common IAM (Identity and Access Management) and PAM (Privileged Access Management) challenges include the following:

1. **Complexity of Hybrid and Multi-Cloud Environments:** Managing identities across on-premises, cloud, and hybrid setups adds layers of complexity, making consistent enforcement difficult.

2. **Integration with Legacy Systems:** Legacy applications and infrastructure often lack support for modern IAM/PAM protocols, creating gaps or requiring custom integrations.

3. **Scaling for Large and Dynamic User Bases:** Supporting thousands of users, including contractors, remote workers, and IoT devices, demands scalable, flexible solutions that are often hard to deploy and manage effectively.

4. **Ensuring User Adoption and Usability:** Security controls like MFA or access restrictions can hinder productivity if not designed with user experience in mind, leading to workarounds or resistance.

5. **Maintaining Least Privilege and Segregation of Duties:** Regularly reviewing and adjusting permissions to align with evolving roles is resource-intensive and often neglected.

6. **Continual Monitoring and Incident Response:** Detecting and responding to privileged account misuse in real-time requires advanced monitoring solutions and skilled personnel.

7. **Balancing Security with Business Needs:** Restrictive access policies can impede operational efficiency, especially in fast-paced or critical environments such as manufacturing or healthcare.

8. **Resource Constraints and Skills Gap:** Implementing, managing, and maintaining effective IAM/PAM systems require specialized expertise that many organizations lack or cannot afford.

9. **Regulatory Compliance and Auditing:** Meeting compliance requirements involves ongoing audits, documentation, and policy enforcement, which can be administratively burdensome.

10. **Detecting and Managing Shadow Identities:** Unauthorized or unmanaged accounts (e.g., service accounts or shadow IT) pose security risks if not properly tracked and controlled.

Addressing these challenges requires strategic planning, automation, user training, and ongoing governance to ensure IAM and PAM systems deliver their intended security benefits without disrupting business operations.

Operational and technical challenges include the following:

- **Complex Environments and Legacy Systems:** Many organizations operate heterogeneous environments with legacy systems that lack modern security features, making integration and enforcement of IAM and PAM policies difficult.

- **User Resistance and Cultural Challenges:** Implementing strict access policies or MFA can face resistance from users accustomed to convenience, leading to workarounds or non-compliance.

- **Scalability:** Organizations with thousands of users and dynamic access needs (e.g., remote/contract workers, IoT devices) face difficulties scaling IAM and PAM solutions efficiently.

- **Balancing Security and Usability:** Overly restrictive controls can hinder productivity, while lax policies increase security risks. Striking a balance requires careful planning.

- **Resource Constraints:** Implementing and maintaining IAM and PAM solutions require skilled personnel, budgeting, and ongoing management, which can be challenging for resource-strapped organizations.

CHAPTER 3   IAM AND PAM RISKS, IMPACTS, AND CHALLENGES

In general, the most used strategies to mitigate risks and address challenges are as follows:

- **Implement Least Privilege and Role-Based Access Controls (RBAC):** Regularly review and limit permissions to the minimum necessary.

- **Enforce Multi-Factor Authentication (MFA):** Protect privileged and sensitive accounts proactively.

- **Automate Lifecycle Management:** Use workflows to revoke or adjust access immediately upon role changes or termination.

- **Continuous Monitoring and Auditing:** Track privileged activities and detect anomalies promptly.

- **Regular Security assessments and Training:** Educate users on secure practices and review IAM/PAM configurations consistently.

- **Adopt Zero Trust Architecture:** Assume no implicit trust and verify every access request dynamically.

Examples of Cybersecurity Attacks Involving IAM and PAM Systems

There have been several high-profile cybersecurity attacks where failures in IAM (Identity and Access Management) and PAM (Privileged Access Management) played a central role.

These incidents highlight how attackers exploit weak access controls, poor credential hygiene, and inadequate privilege monitoring.

Timeline of Major Cybersecurity Attacks Involving IAM and PAM failures is shown in Table 3-1.

Table 3-1. *Timeline of Major Cybersecurity Attacks Involving IAM and PAM Failures*

Year	Incident	Initial Vector	IAM/PAM Failure	Impact
2013	Target	Vendor credential theft	Overprivileged third-party access	40M card records stolen
2020	SolarWinds	Compromised SAML token signing	Lack of PAM on build systems, standing privileges	Thousands of orgs breached APT access
2021	Colonial Pipeline	Stolen VPN credentials, no MFA	Stale accounts, no PAM or MFA on remote access	Fuel pipeline shutdown
2022	Okta (via Sitel)	Vendor compromise	Vendor had standing admin access	Identity platform at risk for customers
2022	Uber	MFA push fatigue + PAM tool compromise	Weak MFA, PAM tool access abused	Access to AWS, Slack, internal tools

Introducing MITRE Att&ck

MITRE ATT&CK (Adversarial Tactics, Techniques, and Common Knowledge) is a **globally accessible knowledge base** of adversary behaviors based on real-world observations. It's used as a **framework for understanding how attackers operate** and helps organizations improve their cybersecurity defenses.

- **Developed by**: MITRE Corporation
- **Purpose**: To categorize and describe common tactics, techniques, and procedures (TTPs) used by cyber adversaries.

- **Structure**: Organized as a **matrix**, where
  - **Tactics** = the **goal** or **objective** of an attacker (e.g., initial access, privilege escalation)
  - **Techniques** = **how** attackers achieve these goals (e.g., phishing, exploiting a vulnerability)
  - **Sub-techniques** = more detailed forms of a technique

Why it matters:
- **Standardizes threat intelligence**: Helps security teams speak a common language.
- **Guides detection and defense**: Aligns detection tools (like SIEM, EDR) to real-world adversary behavior.
- **Supports red/blue/purple teaming**: Used for threat emulation and security validation.
- **Feeds into risk assessments**: Helps evaluate the coverage and effectiveness of your defenses.

Main three MITRE Att&ck iterations are as follows:
1. **Enterprise ATT&CK**: Covers Windows, macOS, Linux, cloud, containers, and mobile platforms.
2. **Mobile ATT&CK**: Specific to iOS and Android.
3. **ICS ATT&CK**: Industrial Control Systems, for OT/SCADA environments.

Main MITRE ATT&CK Matrices

The MITRE ATT&CK Matrix outlines techniques used by adversaries to achieve specific objectives, categorized as tactics. These objectives are presented in a sequence from reconnaissance to exfiltration or the final "impact."

CHAPTER 3   IAM AND PAM RISKS, IMPACTS, AND CHALLENGES

The most comprehensive version is ATT&CK for Enterprise, covering Windows, macOS, Linux, PRE, Azure AD, Office 365, Google Workspace, SaaS, IaaS, networks, and containers.

ATT&CK for Enterprise categorizes adversary tactics and techniques as follows:

1. **Reconnaissance:** Gathering target information for future operations.

2. **Resource Development:** Setting up resources like command infrastructures.

3. **Initial Access:** Gaining network entry, such as through spear phishing.

4. **Execution:** Running malicious code, like remote access tools.

5. **Persistence:** Maintaining access, such as through configuration changes.

6. **Privilege Escalation:** Gaining higher permissions by exploiting vulnerabilities.

7. **Defense Evasion:** Avoiding detection, for example, using trusted processes.

8. **Credential Access:** Stealing usernames and passwords, like with keylogging.

9. **Discovery:** Exploring the environment, identifying control points.

10. **Lateral Movement:** Navigating through systems with legitimate credentials.

11. **Collection:** Gathering data of interest, such as from cloud storage.

12. **Command and Control:** Controlling compromised systems, mimicking normal traffic.

13. **Exfiltration:** Stealing data, transferring it to external locations.

14. **Impact:** Manipulating or destroying systems, like encrypting data with ransomware.

MITRE Att&ck execution flow is shown in Figure 3-1.

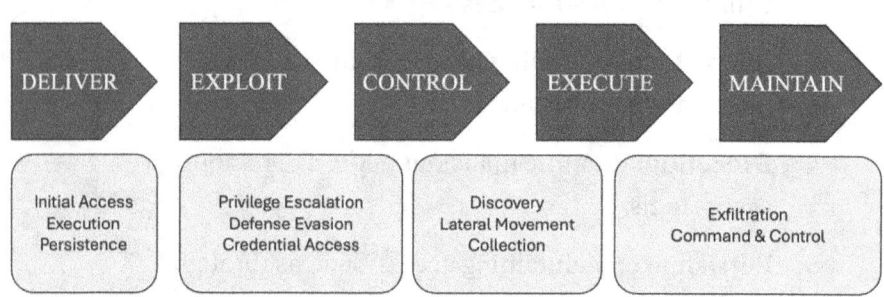

Figure 3-1. *MITRE Att&ck execution flow*

Examples of Mitre Att&ck are shown in Table 3-2.

Table 3-2. *Mitre Att&ck Examples*

Tactic	Technique	Description
Initial Access	Phishing	Sending malicious emails to trick users
Execution	PowerShell	Running scripts to download and execute malware
Lateral Movement	Pass the Hash	Using stolen hashes to move between systems
Exfiltration	Data Transfer to Cloud Storage	Uploading stolen data to attacker-controlled cloud

CHAPTER 3 IAM AND PAM RISKS, IMPACTS, AND CHALLENGES

Mitre Att&ck Mapping for IAM/PAM Exploitation is shown in Table 3-3.

Table 3-3. *Mitre Att&ck Mapping for IAM/PAM Exploitation*

Tactic	Technique ID	Technique Name	Example Use
Initial Access	T1078	Valid Accounts	Using stolen VPN/MFA credentials (Colonial)
Persistence	T1556.004	Modify Authentication Process (SAML abuse)	SolarWinds token forging
Privilege Escalation	T1078.003	Exploitation of Privileged Accounts	Uber PAM compromise
Defense Evasion	T1027	Obfuscated Files or Information	SAML token manipulation
Credential Access	T1552.001	Credentials in Files (scripts, configs)	Hardcoded secrets in PAM-less environments
Lateral Movement	T1021	Remote Services (RDP, SMB, SSH)	Post-compromise privileged session hopping
Command and Control	T1071	Application Layer Protocol	Remote exfiltration of data

Here are some known examples of IAM and PAM cybersecurity attacks.

Example 1: The Capital One Data Breach (2019)

Overview:

In 2019, Capital One experienced a significant data breach that exposed sensitive information of over 100 million customers. The attack was orchestrated through a combination of IAM and access control vulnerabilities.

What happened:

- The attacker exploited a misconfigured web application firewall (WAF) to gain access to Capital One's cloud environment hosted on Amazon Web Services (AWS).

- Using stolen credentials—specifically, an IAM user account that had excessive privileges—the attacker was able to move laterally within the environment. The IAM role permissions allowed the attacker to access customer data stored in AWS S3 buckets.

- The attacker manipulated privileged accounts with broad permissions, exploiting IAM misconfigurations to authorize unauthorized access.

- The attacker used existing privileged credentials to extract data over several months before detection.

Key IAM and PAM Failures:

- **Overly permissive IAM policies:** The compromised IAM user had permissions that should have been restricted or closely monitored.

- **Lack of privilege separation and least privilege enforcement:** The attacker exploited privilege escalation due to insufficient access controls.

- **Inadequate monitoring:** Suspicious activity went unnoticed for months because of ineffective session monitoring and audit logging.

- **Failure to revoke or rotate credentials timely:** Once the breach was detected, remediation was delayed because of unsecured privileged credentials.

Impact:

- Sensitive customer data was exposed, leading to reputational damage and regulatory scrutiny.

- Capital One faced a $80 million fine from US regulators and legal costs.

- The incident underscored the importance of strict IAM and PAM policies, including continuous monitoring, least privilege enforcement, and automated credential management.

Lessons Learned:

- Proper IAM policy configuration and restricting permissions are critical.

- Continuous monitoring and anomaly detection can identify malicious activity early.

- Regular credential rotation and immediate revocation of compromised accounts are vital.

- Strong session logging and audit trails help in post-incident analysis.

Example 2: Hypothetical Cyberattack Scenario in a Manufacturing Plant

Let's see now an example of a detailed hypothetical scenario illustrating how an attack on IAM and PAM systems might occur, tailored to a specific industry.

Background: A manufacturing company relies heavily on Industrial Control Systems (ICS) and Operational Technology (OT) to run their production lines. They use IAM and PAM solutions to control employee and contractor access to both IT and OT systems, with privileged accounts managing critical infrastructure.

Scenario Timeline:

- **Step 1: Reconnaissance and Social Engineering**

    An attacker targets an IT administrator via spear-phishing, sending a convincing email that appears to come from a trusted vendor. The attacker tricks the admin into revealing login credentials or installing malware that captures session tokens.

- **Step 2: Privilege Escalation and Credential Theft**

    Using the compromised admin account, the attacker accesses the PAM console, which manages privileged sessions to OT systems. The attacker extracts privileged account credentials stored within the PAM vault due to weak password policies or inadequate MFA enforcement.

- **Step 3: Unauthorized Access to OT Systems**

    Armed with privileged credentials, the attacker logs into the industrial network via secure remote access tools integrated with IAM policies. Since the IAM

CHAPTER 3   IAM AND PAM RISKS, IMPACTS, AND CHALLENGES

system allows default or shared credentials, and session logging was disabled, the attacker moves laterally within the OT environment undetected.

- **Step 4: Disruption of Manufacturing Processes**

    Using privileged access, the attacker manipulates control parameters, leading to misconfigured machinery. This causes equipment malfunctions, production halts, or safety hazards—leading to costly downtime and safety risks.

- **Step 5: Extraction and Cleanup**

    Before the attack is detected, the attacker covers tracks by deleting session logs and changing access controls. The breach remains hidden for days or weeks, during which sensitive operational data or trade secrets could be stolen.

Key cybersecurity failures in IAM and PAM exploited are as follows:

- **Weak IAM Policy Enforcement:** Overly permissive roles allowed significant lateral movement within systems.

- **Lack of Multi-Factor Authentication:** MFA was not enforced on remote privileged access, enabling credential theft through phishing.

- **Insufficient Privileged Account Management:** Privileged credentials were stored insecurely, with poor rotation policies.

- **No Continuous Monitoring:** Absence of real-time anomaly detection delayed breach detection.

- **Improper Session Controls:** Session logging was disabled or ineffective, making forensic analysis difficult.

Potential impacts involved were the following:

- **Operational Disruption:** Production lines stopped, leading to millions in losses.
- **Safety Risks:** Malicious control changes could potentially cause equipment failures, posing safety hazards.
- **Data Theft:** Trade secrets, process data, and operational blueprints could have been stolen.
- **Regulatory and Reputational Damage:** Regulatory fines, legal actions, and loss of customer trust.

Here is the list of recommendations to be followed in a case like this:

- Enforce **least privilege** policies, limiting privileged access to essential personnel only.
- Implement **multi-factor authentication** for all privileged and remote access sessions.
- Store privileged credentials securely with **automatic rotation** and **audit trails**.
- Use **continuous monitoring** and anomaly detection systems to identify suspicious activities in real time.
- Maintain **strict session recording** and **logging**, ensuring forensic data is retained for investigations.

CHAPTER 3   IAM AND PAM RISKS, IMPACTS, AND CHALLENGES

Example 3: Manufacturing Industry Cyberattack Scenario: Breach via Poor IAM & PAM Controls

Let's see now an example of a cybersecurity breach attack in case of a poor IAM and PAM controls.

Background:

A mid-sized manufacturing company relies on integrated IT and OT systems to operate production lines, manage supply chain data, and control industrial equipment. They use IAM and PAM tools to regulate employee and contractor access, especially for critical control systems.

Here are the typical attack scenario and timeline steps:

- **Step 1: Phishing and Credential Theft**

  An attacker sends a targeted spear-phishing email to an operations technician. The email appears to be from the IT department requesting urgent updates. The technician unwittingly downloads malware that logs keystrokes, capturing the password for the company's privileged account managing the Manufacturing Execution System (MES).

- **Step 2: Privilege Escalation & Gaining Access**

  Using stolen credentials, the attacker logs into the company's PAM portal, which manages privileged access to plant control systems. The company's PAM policy allows shared, baseline privileged accounts with weak passwords and no MFA enforcement for remote access.

105

- **Step 3: Moving Laterally into OT Networks**

  The attacker leverages the compromised privileged credentials to access the Industrial Control System (ICS) network. Since the IAM system failed to enforce strict segmentation and least privilege, the attacker easily navigates into OT systems, gaining control over programmable logic controllers (PLCs).

- **Step 4: Disabling Critical Equipment**

  With privileged access, the attacker manipulates control parameters, disabling safety interlocks and shutting down machinery. This causes a halt in production, risking safety hazards like equipment damage or even workplace injuries.

- **Step 5: Concealing the Intrusion**

  The attacker deletes session logs and creates backdoor accounts through the IAM system, making detection and investigation difficult. Meanwhile, they exfiltrate process data and proprietary manufacturing secrets.

Key Security failures exploited are as follows:

- **Overly Permissive Privileged Accounts:** Shared passwords and weak policies allowed unauthorized access.

- **Lack of MFA on Critical Privileged Accounts:** MFA was not enforced for remote administrator access, making credential theft easier.

- **Poor Network Segmentation:** Lack of sufficient segregation between IT and OT networks enabled lateral movement.

- **Inactive or Excess Privileged Accounts:** Old or unused admin accounts remained active, increasing attack surfaces.

- **No Continuous Monitoring or Alerts:** Absence of real-time activity monitoring delayed breach detection.

Potential Impacts involved were the following:

- **Production Downtime:** The manufacturing process was shut down for 24 hours, costing hundreds of thousands of dollars.

- **Safety Risks:** Malicious reprogramming of control systems could have caused physical damage or worker injuries.

- **Intellectual Property Loss:** Proprietary process data and technical blueprints were stolen.

- **Regulatory and Reputation Damage:** Possible failure to meet safety and cybersecurity standards, risking fines and brand damage.

Here is the list of lessons learned and recommendations to be followed in a case like this:

- **Implement Strict Privilege Policies:** Adopt least privilege principles, restricting account permissions to only what's necessary for the task.

- **Enforce Multi-Factor Authentication (MFA):** Mandate MFA for all remote and high-privilege access, especially for OT and control systems.

- **Segregate Networks and Systems:** Separate IT and OT environments, using firewalls, VPNs, and access controls to limit lateral movement.

- **Vote for Regular Access Reviews:** Perform frequent audits on privilege accounts—disable or delete unused accounts immediately.

- **Implement Real-Time Monitoring:** Use SIEM tools to detect anomalies such as unusual access times, large data transfers, or command executions on control devices.

- **Secure Credential Storage and Rotation:** Use privileged credential vaults with automatic rotations to prevent credential reuse and theft.

The Future of Identity and Access Management (IAM) and Privileged Access Management (PAM)

The future of Identity and Access Management (IAM) and Privileged Access Management (PAM) will be shaped by evolving technologies, increasing cyber threats, and the ongoing need for robust security policies.

Key risks include the rise of advanced persistent threats (APTs) that develop more targeted and stealthy methods to bypass IAM and PAM controls, as well as the persistent threat of credential theft and misuse, especially targeting privileged accounts.

The reliance on third-party vendors and cloud services introduces additional vulnerabilities if proper access controls are not enforced, while insider threats—whether malicious or negligent—remain a significant concern, particularly in remote or hybrid work environments.

Legacy systems lacking modern security features also continue to pose vulnerabilities. The impacts of these risks may result in operational disruptions, data loss, reputation damage, regulatory penalties, and substantial financial costs. Addressing these challenges requires balancing strong security measures with usability, managing identities across increasingly complex and diverse environments such as cloud, IoT, and hybrid systems, and providing real-time, context-aware access controls.

Organizations will also need to navigate the risks associated with automating and deploying AI-driven security tools, as well as overcoming skills shortages in cybersecurity expertise. Looking ahead, a shift toward Zero Trust architectures emphasizing continuous verification, least privilege, and micro-segmentation is expected to become standard practice.

Decentralized identity models using blockchain technology, widespread adoption of biometric authentication, and the integration of AI and machine learning to enhance threat detection and response are poised to transform the landscape. Additionally, evolving regulatory frameworks will continue to push organizations to strengthen their identity security measures, making effective IAM and PAM strategies more critical than ever for protecting digital assets, ensuring compliance, and maintaining trust in an increasingly interconnected world.

Summary

In this chapter, we described the most common **Identity and Access Management (IAM)** and **Privileged Access Management (PAM)** risks which include misconfigurations, lack of visibility, overprovisioning and weak controls.

Also we discussed which best practices to apply to mitigate the cybersecurity risks for both IAM and PAM including enforcing **least privilege** and **just-in-time access**, making sure to automate **provisioning/ deprovisioning** and **access reviews**; always using **MFA**, especially for privileged accounts; implementing **session recording**, **vaulting**, and **audit trails;** and always monitoring for **anomalies** and **access abuse**.

CHAPTER 3   IAM AND PAM RISKS, IMPACTS, AND CHALLENGES

We analyze the based on risks, which are the most common **impacts**, and **Operational challenges associated with IAM and PAM in Modern Cybersecurity**.

We then provided some examples of **Cybersecurity attacks involving IAM and PAM systems** where failures in IAM (Identity and Access Management) and PAM (Privileged Access Management) played a central role.

Finally, as on the major and moder cybersecurity attack the **MITRE Att&ck** was fully explained.

CHAPTER 4

IAM and PAM Tools, Standards and Frameworks

In the previous chapter, we described the major IAM and PAM risks, impacts, and challenges and in particular what are the major Access Management risks, impacts, and challenges, like Unauthorized Access, Credential Theft and Identity Spoofing, Insider Threats, etc., and how to solve and remediate them with robust IAM and PAM solutions.

In today's growing digital era, managing access to critical information and resources is more crucial than ever. Identity and Access Management (IAM) and Privileged Access Management (PAM) are pivotal in safeguarding an organization's data against unauthorized access and potential breaches.

IAM focuses on ensuring that only the right individuals have appropriate access to technology resources, while PAM specifically manages and monitors privileged access, which involves elevated permission levels.

Implementing robust IAM and PAM solutions not only enhances security but also streamlines compliance with various regulatory standards. IAM and PAM tools are designed to align with key frameworks and standards, providing a structured approach to access management.

CHAPTER 4   IAM AND PAM TOOLS, STANDARDS AND FRAMEWORKS

IAM and PAM tools, standards, and frameworks offer a structured approach to managing identities, ensuring privileged access is secure, and helping organizations comply with regulatory requirements.

This chapter delves into the essential tools, industry standards, and frameworks that empower organizations to protect their digital assets effectively and maintain a secure and compliant environment.

So, which IAM and PAM tools, standards, and framework should be considered? Which are the most commonly used?

IAM tools like Microsoft Azure Active Directory (Azure AD), Okta, Ping Identity, ForgeRock, etc., will be introduced.

PAM tools like SSH PrivX IT/OT, CyberArk Privileged Access Security, BeyondTrust Privileged Management, Delinea, Wallix, Claroty, etc., will be discussed.

As IAM and PAM frameworks, we will concentrate for instance on NIST Cybersecurity Framework (NIST CSF), Zero Trust Architecture, ISO/IEC 27001 and 27002.

Finally, as IAM and PAM standards for IT and OT we will discuss about ISO/IEC 27001 and 27002, NIST SP 800-53, IEC 62443, and NIST SP 800-63.

Let's review now in detail IAM and PAM **Tools, Frameworks, and Standards.**

Introduction to IAM and PAM Tools

Together, IAM and PAM tools enhance security and compliance by ensuring proper access controls and protecting critical systems from unauthorized use.

Let's remind the most important purpose, function, and a simple example of the IAM and PAM tools and how and why they are both critical components of a comprehensive cybersecurity strategy, especially in environments with high compliance requirements and sensitive assets.

Implementing both IAM and PAM solutions strategically allows organizations to safeguard their entire digital and operational environment, controlling access at every level while monitoring privileged activities to prevent insider and external threats.

Identity and Access Management (IAM) Tools:

- **Purpose:** Manage user identities and regulate access to systems and data.

- **Functions:** User provisioning, authentication, and role management.

- **Examples:** Okta, Microsoft Azure AD, etc.

Privileged Access Management (PAM) Tools:

- **Purpose:** Secure and control access to privileged accounts with elevated permissions.

- **Functions:** Credential vaulting, session recording, and just-in-time access.

- **Examples:** SSH Communications Security, CyberArk, BeyondTrust, etc.

Let's first start to see the key benefits of IAM and PAM tools, which create a secure environment where access is carefully controlled, monitored, and audited to protect against unauthorized activities and ensure data integrity.

General key benefits of IAM and PAM tools include the following:

- **Enhanced Security:** Both tools protect sensitive information and critical infrastructure by enforcing strict access controls.

- **Compliance Support:** It helps meet regulatory requirements such as GDPR, HIPAA, and SOX by providing audit trails and access logs.

- **Operational Efficiency:** It automates and streamlines access management processes, reducing administrative burdens and human errors.

- **Reduced Risk:** By effectively managing identities and privileges, organizations lower the risk of insider threats and cyberattacks.

Let's elaborate the key benefits of IAM and PAM tools.

Identity and Access Management (IAM) tools' key benefits include the following:

1. **Centralized Access Control:** IAM provides a unified platform to manage identities, credentials, roles, and policies across various systems—cloud, on-premises, and hybrid. This centralized approach ensures consistency in enforcement and simplifies security operations.

2. **Improved Regulatory Compliance:** IAM tools help organizations comply with data protection and cybersecurity regulations (e.g., GDPR, HIPAA, SOX, NIS2). They enable precise access records, enforce data minimization, and generate reports required for audits.

3. **Risk Reduction Through Least Privilege:** By enforcing the principle of least privilege, IAM ensures users only have the permissions necessary for their roles. This minimizes the attack surface and mitigates the impact of compromised accounts.

4. **Efficient Onboarding and Offboarding:** Automated identity lifecycle management streamlines how users are added and removed. Quick provisioning

helps with productivity, while swift deprovisioning helps eliminate orphaned accounts that pose security risks.

5. **Enhanced User Experience and Security:** IAM integrates features like Single Sign-On (SSO), federated identity, and Multi-Factor Authentication (MFA), offering secure, seamless access while reducing password fatigue and improving user adoption.

Privileged Access Management (PAM) tools' key benefits include the following:

1. **Protection of Critical Systems and Assets:** PAM tools isolate and manage access to high-value systems and sensitive data, ensuring that only authorized users with verified credentials can perform privileged actions.

2. **Granular Control and Just-in-Time Access:** Access to privileged accounts can be fine-tuned to specific time windows, systems, or operations. Just-in-Time (JIT) provisioning and ephemeral access reduce standing privileges and associated risks.

3. **Full Visibility and Auditability:** All privileged sessions can be monitored, recorded, and logged for review. This provides a forensic trail for detecting abuse or responding to incidents—essential for compliance and incident response.

4. **Reduced Attack Surface:** Credential vaulting, password rotation, and automatic privilege revocation reduce the chances of credentials being reused, leaked, or stolen—especially by malware or insiders.

5. **Compliance with Security Frameworks:** PAM aligns with regulatory and industry frameworks such as IEC 62443 (for OT), ISO 27001, PCI DSS, and NIS2. It supports required security controls around access governance and auditability.

Table 4-1 shows a comparison for highlighting the key differences and strategic considerations for deploying IAM and PAM tools.

Table 4-1. IAM vs. PAM Comparison Table and Deployment Strategies

Aspect	IAM (Identity and Access Management)	PAM (Privileged Access Management)
Focus Area	Manage general user identities and access to resources	Secure and monitor privileged, high-level accounts
Scope	All organizational users, employees, partners, customers	Privileged users/accounts with elevated permissions
Key Features	SSO, MFA, user lifecycle management, federation, RBAC	Password vaulting, session recording, activity monitoring
Typical Use Cases	Onboarding/offboarding employees, application access, B2E (Business-to-Employee)	Critical systems, admin access, remote privileged sessions
Security Objective	Ensure correct access, reduce credential fatigue	Prevent privilege misuse, insider threats, audit trails
Implementation Challenges	Managing large user populations, integrating multiple systems	Securing legacy systems, privileged session oversight
Deployment Strategies	Centralized management, integrate with HR systems, adopt single sign-on	Secure privileged pathways, automate credential rotation, monitor privileged activities
Ideal Environments	Large enterprises with diverse apps and cloud services	Environments with high sensitivity, compliance needs, or legacy OT systems

Deployment best practices of IAM and PAM tools include the following:

For IAM:

- Start with a comprehensive inventory of user identities and access rights.

- Implement Role-Based Access Control (RBAC) to streamline permissions.

- Enforce multi-factor authentication (MFA) for critical and remote access.
- Integrate IAM with HR systems for automated onboarding and offboarding.
- Adopt a Zero Trust approach: verify every access request continuously.

For PAM:

- Discover and inventory all privileged accounts across systems.
- Use privileged session management to record and monitor activity.
- Automate password rotation and enforce strict access policies.
- Limit the number of users with privileged access (least privilege).
- Conduct regular audits and compliance reporting.

Introduction to IAM and PAM Tools Vendors

Here is a short introduction of the IAM and PAM vendors who are widely recognized for their mature solutions, extensive feature sets, and integration capabilities across diverse IT and OT environments (source: Gartner).

Top IAM leading Vendors:

1. **Okta**: Offers cloud-based identity management, Single Sign-On (SSO), Multi-Factor Authentication (MFA), and lifecycle management.

2. **Microsoft Azure Active Directory (Azure AD)**: Provides comprehensive cloud IAM, integrating seamlessly with Microsoft services and enterprise applications.

CHAPTER 4 IAM AND PAM TOOLS, STANDARDS AND FRAMEWORKS

3. **Ping Identity:** Known for flexible identity federation, SSO, MFA, and cloud-native IAM solutions.

4. **IBM:** Comprehensive, enterprise-grade security solutions that integrate advanced identity management, AI-driven analytics, and seamless cloud.

Table 4-2 shows a comparison of top key IAM vendors.

Table 4-2. A Comparison of Top Key IAM Vendors

Vendor	Core Features	Strengths	Use Cases
Okta	SSO, MFA, user provisioning, lifecycle management, API security	Extensive integrations, ease of use	Cloud applications, hybrid environments
Microsoft Azure AD	SSO, identity protection, conditional access, B2B/B2C identity services	Seamless Microsoft ecosystem integration	Enterprises using Microsoft products
Ping Identity	Secure SSO, adaptive MFA, federated identity, API security	Strong for complex environments	Large enterprises, hybrid IT architectures
IBM	SSO, MFA, user provisioning, identity protection, lifecycle management, API security, federated identity, API security	Extensive integrations, ease of use, Scalable, flexible deployment options and Strong for complex environments	Large enterprises, Cloud applications, hybrid environments, AI enhanced threat detection

Top PAM leading vendors for IT:

1. **CyberArk**
   - Industry leader in privileged account security with features like credential management, session monitoring, and threat analytics.

2. **BeyondTrust**
   - Provides unified PAM solutions including password management, session recordings, and threat detection.

3. **Delinea (formerly Thycotic)**
   - Simplifies privileged account management with automation, secret management, and audit features.

4. **Centrify (Delinea)**
   - Focuses on securing hybrid and cloud environments with privileged access controls and multi-cloud support.

Table 4-3 shows a comparison of top key PAM vendors for IT.

CHAPTER 4   IAM AND PAM TOOLS, STANDARDS AND FRAMEWORKS

Table 4-3. *A Comparison of Top Key PAM Vendors*

Vendor	Core Features	Strengths	Use Cases
CyberArk	Privileged account security, session management, threat analytics	Comprehensive PAM suite, strong security	Large enterprises, critical infrastructure
BeyondTrust	Password vaulting, session monitoring, least privilege enforcement	Unified PAM platform, ease of deployment	Enterprises needing integrated solutions
Delinea (Thycotic & Centrify)	Secret management, session recording, access control, role-based access	User-friendly, scalable	Hybrid and multi-cloud environments

For OT-focused PAM vendors for both IT and OT, **SSH Communications Security** is one of the companies known for providing a modern, secure, scalable PAM solution for converging IT/OT data and systems. The solution is named **PrivX OT PAM**, which is a secure access management solution for industrial automation and manufacturing businesses that require access management at scale.

Major benefits of SSH PrivX OT PAM solution include the following:

- Integrates with IT/OT systems
- Industrial (remote) access to modern/legacy ICS targets in hybrid environments
- Local/remote troubleshooting and data collection
- Least-privilege and just-enough-access (not available with VPNs and firewalls)
- Grants just-in-time Zero Trust access to industrial targets

CHAPTER 4   IAM AND PAM TOOLS, STANDARDS AND FRAMEWORKS

SSH PrivX-offered IT/OT PAM solution is shown in Figure 4-1.

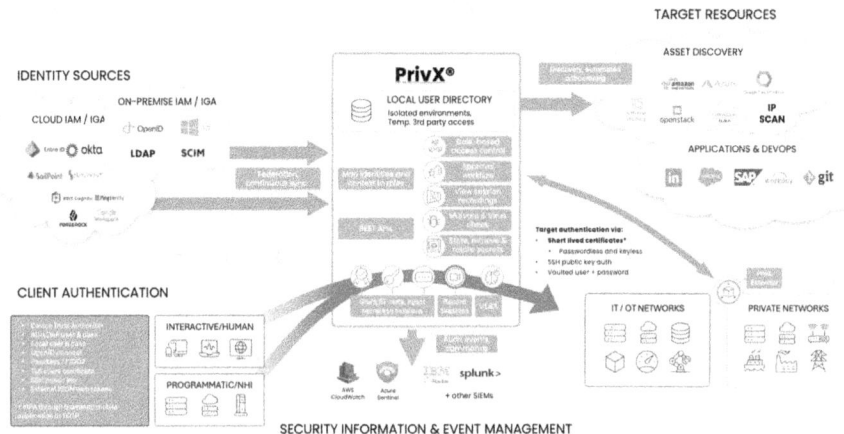

Figure 4-1. *SSH PrivX IT/OT PAM solution overview*

Figure 4-2 shows the SSH PrivX OT solution access methods such as the following:

1. Access to typical IT sources like Servers, Network devices, DBs, Applications, etc.

2. Access to OT-specific resources like PLC, HMI, etc. via Jump host Server.

3. Access to OT-specific resources such as services, systems, or subnets, which are accessed using arbitrary TCP/IP protocols.

CHAPTER 4   IAM AND PAM TOOLS, STANDARDS AND FRAMEWORKS

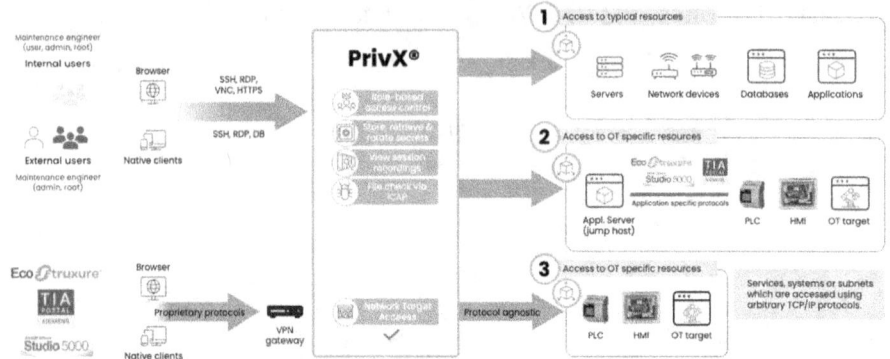

Figure 4-2. SSH PrivX OT PAM access methods

Introduction to IAM and PAM Frameworks

Organizations looking to secure digital access should adopt both IAM and PAM frameworks. By leveraging well-established standards like RBAC, SAML, and OAuth, and integrating leading tools like Microsoft Entra ID, Okta, CyberArk, and BeyondTrust, companies can build a layered and effective access control architecture.

Here's a detailed overview of **common IAM** and **PAM frameworks**, including widely adopted **standards**, **models**, and **solutions** used by organizations to implement identity and privileged access management.

Common IAM frameworks that help manage digital identities, authentication are shown in Tables 4-4 and 4-5.

Table 4-4. Standards and Models in IAM

Framework/Standard	Description
RBAC (Role-Based Access Control)	Grants access based on a user's role within an organization. Roles are assigned specific permissions.
ABAC (Attribute-Based Access Control)	Access is granted based on attributes (e.g., user location, time of day, device). Offers more flexibility than RBAC.
OpenID Connect (OIDC)	An identity layer built on top of OAuth 2.0 for user authentication in web and mobile apps.
SAML (Security Assertion Markup Language)	Enables Single Sign-On (SSO) between identity providers and service providers.
OAuth 2.0	A protocol for access delegation (commonly used to grant third-party applications access without sharing passwords).
FIDO2/WebAuthn	Passwordless authentication standards using biometrics or hardware tokens.

Table 4-5. Common IAM Tools and Platforms

Tool	Description
Microsoft Entra ID (formerly Azure AD)	Enterprise identity and access solution supporting SSO, MFA, and conditional access for Microsoft and non-Microsoft apps.
Okta	Cloud-based IAM offering user provisioning, SSO, MFA, and API access management.
Auth0	Developer-friendly identity platform for building IAM features into apps.

(continued)

CHAPTER 4   IAM AND PAM TOOLS, STANDARDS AND FRAMEWORKS

Table 4-5. (*continued*)

Tool	Description
Ping Identity	Enterprise-grade identity management platform with support for SSO, MFA, and federation.
ForgeRock	Comprehensive IAM suite with identity governance, access management, and directory services.
IBM Security Verify	Offers IAM solutions for cloud, hybrid, and on-prem environments with AI-enhanced threat detection.

Common PAM frameworks, shown in Tables 4-6 and 4-7, focus on managing, monitoring, and securing privileged accounts that have elevated permissions in systems and applications.

Table 4-6. *Standards and Concepts in PAM*

Framework/Concept	Description
Principle of Least Privilege	Users and systems get the minimum access necessary to perform their tasks.
Just-in-Time (JIT) Access	Temporary elevation of privileges for a limited time based on user requests or policies.
Privileged Session Management (PSM)	Monitoring and recording sessions initiated by privileged accounts.
Credential Vaulting	Securely stores and rotates passwords or keys for privileged accounts.
Zero Standing Privileges (ZSP)	No user retains permanent admin rights; access is granted dynamically when needed.

Table 4-7. Common PAM Tools and Platforms

Tool	Description
CyberArk	Industry-leading PAM solution offering credential vaulting, session monitoring, and threat analytics.
BeyondTrust	Offers endpoint privilege management, password vaulting, and session recording.
Thycotic (now Delinea)	Provides cloud-ready PAM tools with strong usability and scalable architecture.
One Identity Safeguard	Unified PAM solution integrating session monitoring and access controls.
IBM Security Verify Privilege Vault	Enterprise-grade password vault with session control capabilities.
ManageEngine PAM360	Integrated PAM offering account discovery, password management, and auditing.

Pros and Cons of IAM and PAM Frameworks

There are of course pros and cons of IAM and PAM. IAM's pros and cons are shown in Table 4-8.

Table 4-8. IAM's Pros and Cons

Pros	Cons
Centralizes user identity and access control across the organization	May not adequately cover privileged accounts without PAM
Improves user productivity with SSO and self-service options	Complex to implement across legacy or hybrid environments
Reduces password fatigue via federation and MFA	Risk of SSO compromise if MFA isn't enforced
Supports compliance through auditing and access governance	Requires ongoing policy updates and identity lifecycle management
Can integrate with HR systems for automatic provisioning	Needs strong role design (RBAC) to avoid over-permissioning

PAM's pros and cons are shown in Table 4-9.

Table 4-9. PAM's Pros and Cons

Pros	Cons
Protects the most sensitive and high-risk assets	Often more expensive and complex to deploy than IAM
Reduces insider threat and credential misuse	User resistance due to more restrictions or monitoring
Enforces least privilege and ephemeral access	Poor integration with IAM leads to silos
Enables compliance with stricter regulations (e.g., PCI, NIST)	May need manual fine-tuning of access workflows
Records and audits all privileged sessions for forensic review	Performance overhead if not configured properly

CHAPTER 4   IAM AND PAM TOOLS, STANDARDS AND FRAMEWORKS

Let's now introduce IAM and PAM security standards.

IAM and PAM are integral components of a robust cybersecurity strategy. By adhering to international standards and best practices, organizations can better protect their assets from unauthorized access and compliance breaches. As cyber threats evolve, so too should the frameworks and tools used to manage identities and privileges, ensuring a proactive approach to cybersecurity.

From a cybersecurity perspective, inadequate IAM and PAM controls significantly raise the risk of successful cyberattacks, exploitation, and lateral movement within networks.

These lead to severe impacts like data theft, operational shutdowns, ransomware infections, regulatory fines, and reputational damage.

Robust standards, continuous monitoring, and incident preparedness are essential to mitigate these evolving threats.

Weak IAM and PAM controls pose significant risks, including data theft, operational outages, financial penalties, and damage to reputation. Implementing robust standards and continuous monitoring mitigates these risks and ensures long-term security and resilience.

Here are the most common IAM security standards:

- **ISO/IEC 27001:**

    - **Overview:** A global standard for information security management systems (ISMS). It provides a systematic approach to managing sensitive company information.

    - **Access Management Specifics:** Includes requirements for creating an access control policy, user access management, and user responsibilities.

    - **Benefits:** Helps organizations protect data systematically, ensuring confidentiality, integrity, and availability.

CHAPTER 4   IAM AND PAM TOOLS, STANDARDS AND FRAMEWORKS

- **NIST SP 800-53:**
  - **Overview:** A comprehensive set of guidelines for federal information systems, including security and privacy controls.
  - **Access Management Specifics:** Recommends controls for identity verification, account management, and least privilege.
  - **Benefits:** Enhances risk management processes and helps meet compliance requirements for federal agencies.
- **GDPR (General Data Protection Regulation):**
  - **Overview:** A regulation in the EU focusing on data protection and privacy.
  - **Access Management Specifics:** Requires organizations to implement strict access controls to protect personal data, including data minimization and purpose limitation.
  - **Benefits:** Enhances data protection for individuals, with stringent requirements and heavy penalties for non-compliance.

PAM security standards include the following:

- **ISO/IEC 27002:**
  - **Overview:** Provides guidelines for executing security controls listed in ISO/IEC 27001.
  - **Privileged Access Specifics:** Emphasizes secure password policies, monitoring and auditing of privileged user activities, and protection of sensitive data.

CHAPTER 4   IAM AND PAM TOOLS, STANDARDS AND FRAMEWORKS

- **Benefits:** Supports the design and implementation of effective security controls for privileged accounts.

- **NIST Cybersecurity Framework:**

  - **Overview:** A voluntary framework that provides a policy framework of computer security guidance for how private sector organizations can assess and improve their ability to prevent, detect, and respond to cyber-attacks.

  - **Privileged Access Specifics:** Recommends identifying, protecting, detecting, and responding to threats associated with privileged accounts.

  - **Benefits:** Helps organizations align their cybersecurity measures with business needs and regulatory requirements.

- **SOX (Sarbanes-Oxley Act):**

  - **Overview:** US law aimed at protecting investors by improving the accuracy and reliability of corporate disclosures.

  - **Privileged Access Specifics:** Imposes requirements for internal controls and reporting, emphasizing the need for strict access measures and audit trails for financial reporting systems.

  - **Benefits:** Reduces risk of fraud and improves the reliability of financial reporting.

CHAPTER 4   IAM AND PAM TOOLS, STANDARDS AND FRAMEWORKS

Table 4-10 shows a comparison of IAM and PAM standards, and it highlights the focus, scope, and key aspects of access and privileged access management across different standards. It aims to provide a clear comparison, helping organizations choose the standards that best fit their needs, whether for compliance, security enhancement, or specific operational requirements.

Table 4-10. A Comparison of IAM and PAM Standards

Feature/Standard	ISO/IEC 27001	NIST SP 800-53	GDPR	ISO/IEC 27002	NIST Cybersecurity Framework	SOX
Focus	Information security management systems	Security and privacy controls	Data protection and privacy	Guidelines for security controls	Cybersecurity guidance	Financial reporting and internal controls
Scope	Global, applicable to all industries	Federal information systems	European data protection regulation	Supporting ISO/IEC 27001	Voluntary framework for organizations	U.S. publicly traded companies
Access Management	Access control policy, user access	Identity and access management	Data minimization, access limitation	Privileged access security	Access controls and identity verification	Internal controls over access and reporting
Privileged Access	User responsibilities, access control	Account management, least privilege	Protection of personal data	Password policies, audit logs	Protecting privileged access	Requires strict audit trails
Compliance	Certification available	Compliance for federal agencies	Mandatory for EU compliance	Supports implementation of ISO 27001	Aligns security with business needs	Legal requirement for financial compliance
Benefits	Systematic data protection	Enhanced risk management	Strong data protection, heavy penalties	Effective control implementation	Framework for risk reduction	Fraud reduction, reliable reporting

Some of the standards that we just introduced are fundamental for IT cybersecurity compliance.

Table 4-11 shows a compliance checklist based on NIST, IEC 62443, and NIS2.

CHAPTER 4   IAM AND PAM TOOLS, STANDARDS AND FRAMEWORKS

Table 4-11. *A Compliance Checklist*

Requirement Area	Standards/Guidelines	Actions/Controls
Identity Verification	NIST SP 800-53, NIST 800-63	MFA for all privileged/remote access; identity proofing processes.
Privileged Credential Security	IEC 62443-4-2, NIST SP 800-53	Store credentials in secure vaults; rotate passwords regularly; restrict access.
Network Segmentation	IEC 62443-2-4, NIS2	Segregate OT from IT; enforce least privilege on network access.
Monitoring & Logging	NIST SP 800-137, IEC 62443-3-3	Implement comprehensive logging; monitor logs continuously; retain logs for audit.
Incident Response	NIST SP 800-61	Develop and test incident response plans; include privileged account misuse scenarios.
Supply Chain Security	IEC 62443-4-2, NIS2	Vet third-party access; enforce secure credentials management.

Implementing IAM and PAM Standards

By understanding and implementing these standards, organizations can strengthen their IAM and PAM processes, enhancing overall security and compliance.

To effectively utilize these standards

- **Conduct Regular Audits:** Ensure compliance by regularly reviewing access controls and security measures.

CHAPTER 4   IAM AND PAM TOOLS, STANDARDS AND FRAMEWORKS

- **Automate Processes:** Use tools that support standards compliance, providing continuous monitoring and reporting.

- **Develop Policies:** Align security policies with standards, ensuring clear guidance for managing identities and privileges.

- **Employee Training:** Regularly update and educate staff on compliance requirements and security best practices.

Let's highlight the pros and cons of IAM and PAM security standards in Table 4-12.

Table 4-12. Pros and Cons of IAM and PAM Security Standards

Standard	Pros	Cons
ISO/IEC 27001	• Globally recognized; provides a comprehensive framework • Facilitates certification • Focuses on continuous improvement	• Can be resource-intensive to implement • Requires ongoing audits and maintenance
NIST SP 800-53	• Extensive controls tailored for federal and critical infrastructure • Good for risk management • Supports diverse organizational needs	• Complex and detailed, may be challenging for small organizations • Heavy documentation workload

(continued)

Table 4-12. (*continued*)

Standard	Pros	Cons
GDPR	• Strong focus on personal data protection • Can improve customer trust • Mandates strict access controls	• Compliance can be costly and complex • Heavy penalties for violations
ISO/IEC 27002	• Practical guidelines to implement ISO/IEC 27001 controls • Widely adopted good practices	• Not certifiable on its own • Needs to be integrated with broader ISMS framework
NIST Cybersecurity Framework	• Flexible and adaptable for all sectors • Emphasizes a risk-based approach • Promotes continuous improvement	• Not prescriptive–requires customization • May lack specific technical guidance
SOX	• Strong internal control mandates • Improves financial transparency and accountability • Can reduce fraud risk	• Adds compliance overhead and costs • Focuses mainly on financial data–limited scope for broader security controls

CHAPTER 4   IAM AND PAM TOOLS, STANDARDS AND FRAMEWORKS

The key benefits of implementing IAM and PAM standards are shown in Table 4-13.

Table 4-13. *The Key Benefits of Implementing IAM and PAM Standards*

Benefit	Description
Enhanced Security	Strong access controls and privileged account management reduce the risk of unauthorized access, insider threats, and cyberattacks.
Regulatory Compliance	Helps organizations meet legal and regulatory requirements such as GDPR, SOX, NIST, and ISO standards, avoiding penalties and fines.
Risk Management	Systematic identification, assessment, and mitigation of risks related to identity and privilege access.
Operational Efficiency	Automation of user provisioning, de-provisioning, and credential management streamlines workflows and reduces administrative burden.
Auditability and Accountability	Clear logs, audit trails, and monitoring ensure accountability and facilitate security audits and incident investigations.
Data Confidentiality and Integrity	Proper identity and privilege controls protect sensitive data from leaks and tampering.
User Productivity	Seamless and secure access mechanisms (like Single Sign-On, MFA) improve user experience and reduce login friction.
Resilience and Incident Response	Structured access controls and continuous monitoring improve organizations' ability to detect, respond to, and recover from security incidents.
Confidence to Stakeholders	Demonstrates strong security posture to customers, partners, and regulators, boosting trust and reputation.

CHAPTER 4   IAM AND PAM TOOLS, STANDARDS AND FRAMEWORKS

Table 4-14 shows a summary of **risks** and **impacts** associated with inadequate or poorly implemented IAM and PAM frameworks.

Table 4-14. *Risk and Impacts of IAM and PAM Frameworks*

Risks	Description	Impacts	Description
Unauthorized Access	Attackers or insiders gaining access to sensitive systems and data.	Data Breach	Loss of confidential information leading to legal, financial, and reputational damage.
Privilege Escalation	Exploiting system vulnerabilities to gain higher access rights.	System Disruption	Disruption of operations, potential damage to industrial or critical infrastructure systems.
Credential Theft	Stealing user or privileged account credentials via phishing, malware, or insider abuse.	Financial Loss & Penalties	Direct financial theft, regulatory fines, and legal consequences.
Insider Threats	Malicious or negligent actions by employees with privileged access.	Data Destruction, Theft, Sabotage	Loss of IP, operational downtime, safety hazards, and compliance violations.
Non-Compliance Penalties	Failing to meet standards like GDPR, SOX, or NIST leads to legal repercussions.	Fines & Sanctions	Heavy penalties, increased regulatory scrutiny, and reputational harm.
Operational Disruption	Uncontrolled access leading to system misconfigurations or shutdowns.	Business Interruptions	Reduced productivity and increased downtime affecting revenue and service delivery.
Reputational Damage	Publicized breaches erode stakeholder trust.	Customer Loss	Long-term loss of business opportunities and brand value.

As we described in detail in Chapter 3, weak IAM and PAM controls pose significant risks, including data theft, operational outages, financial penalties, and damage to reputation. Implementing robust standards and continuous monitoring mitigates these risks and ensures long-term security and resilience.

From a cybersecurity perspective, inadequate IAM and PAM controls significantly raise the risk of successful cyberattacks, exploitation, and lateral movement within networks. These lead to severe impacts like data theft, operational shutdowns, ransomware infections, regulatory fines, and reputational damage. Robust standards, continuous monitoring, and incident preparedness are essential to mitigate these evolving threats.

A detailed example or recommendations on risk mitigation strategies from cybersecurity perspective are discussed in Chapter 3, but here is a recap of the focused summary of cybersecurity risks and impacts associated with weak or insufficient IAM and PAM controls as shown in Table 4-15.

CHAPTER 4   IAM AND PAM TOOLS, STANDARDS AND FRAMEWORKS

Table 4-15. *Summary of Cybersecurity Risks and Impacts*

Cybersecurity Risks	Description	Impacts	Description
Unauthorized Access & Data Breaches	Attackers exploiting weak authentication or privilege controls to access sensitive systems/data.	Data Leakage & Corruption	Loss or alteration of critical data, leading to operational chaos and potential compliance violations.
Privilege Escalation & Lateral Movement	Attackers using exploited credentials to move deeper into the network and access critical assets.	System Disruption & Downtime	Disruption of normal operations, equipment damage, and possible physical safety hazards in OT environments.
Credential Theft & Phishing Attacks	Cybercriminals stealing credentials via phishing, malware, or social engineering.	Rapid Spread of Malware/Ransomware	Ransomware or malware can propagate quickly, locking down systems and causing financial and operational damages.
Insider Threats & Malicious Actions	Insider actors abusing privileged access either maliciously or negligently.	Insider Data Theft or Sabotage	Intellectual property loss, safety risks, and operational sabotage damaging trust and productivity.
Weak Monitoring & Incident Response	Ineffective logging and monitoring delay threat detection and response.	Extended Exploitation & Larger Breaches	Attackers can stay undetected longer, increasing the scope and impact of breaches, with higher recovery costs.
Non-Compliance with Security Standards	Failing to meet security standards like IEC 62443, NIST, or NIS2 increases vulnerability.	Regulatory Penalties & Increased Attack Surface	Fines, legal actions, and increased attack attractiveness for cybercriminals due to poor security posture.

Summary

In this chapter, we described why the implementation of secure and robust IAM and PAM solutions not only enhances security but also streamlines compliance with various regulatory standards, tools, and framework empowering organizations to protect their digital assets effectively and maintain a secure and compliant environment.

So, we started introducing which IAM and PAM tools, standards, and framework should be considered and of course which of them are mostly used and why.

CHAPTER 4   IAM AND PAM TOOLS, STANDARDS AND FRAMEWORKS

We discussed the IAM tools like Microsoft Azure Active Directory (Azure AD), Okta, Ping Identity, ForgeRock, etc., as well as PAM tools like SSH PrivX IT/OT, CyberArk Privileged Access Security, BeyondTrust Privileged Management, Delinea, Wallix, Claroty, etc.

Then we moved to frameworks and discussed what are the most used and why.

As IAM and PAM frameworks, we will concentrate for instance on NIST Cybersecurity Framework (NIST CSF), Zero Trust Architecture, ISO/IEC 27001 & 27002.

We introduced finally, of course, the most common IAM and PAM standards for both IT and OT environments and pointed out the major differences. The most common are ISO/IEC 27001 & 27002, NIST SP 800-53, IEC 62443, and NIST SP 800-63.